T0321289

Mark Rutland

Keep On Keeping On

 CHARISMA HOUSE

DEDICATION

Grow old along with me!
The best is yet to be,
The last of life, for which the first was
    made:
Our times are in His hand
Who saith "A whole I planned,
Youth shows but half; trust God: see
    all, nor be afraid!"
          —ROBERT BROWNING

As OF THIS writing my wife, Alison, and I have been married fifty-seven years. We first met in junior high school, she in the eighth grade and I in the ninth. I do not think they still call those grades junior high. In fact, almost nothing is still called what it was called then.

What a little beauty she was in the eighth grade. You can believe this or not, but for me it was literally love at first sight. I was new at her school, which was nothing new to me. My family moved habitually. We were like Mongol herdsmen always in search of better pastures.

The first time I laid eyes on her I turned to the boy next to me and said, "I am going to marry that girl."

It was hardly the impetuous and reckless comment of a mere boy, for though she was only in the eighth grade, I was much older and far more mature being in the ninth grade. Impetuous or not, I never backed down. Five years later, at the ripe old ages of seventeen and nineteen, we were married. I have never for even a fleeting moment regretted the pursuit and capture of such a lovely creature as she.

I know, and this is not false humility, there have been moments, very serious moments, when she thought she must have had rocks in her head. Perhaps she did, but it fell out to my good. She asked me recently what I thought my life would have been had I married someone else. Brief, I said, and miserable. I am alive today and happy in God because of her. Everyone second guesses themselves occasionally. She has been, since the first moment she entered my field of vision, the only totally unregretted and un-rethought decision of my life.

She has been my co-laborer in ministry, in missions, in pastoring, and in the leadership of two universities. She was there for every mile, or else she was at home raising our children. She and I taught together and spoke at conferences, youth camps, and marriage seminars together. Together. All the accomplishments. All the stress. My failures. Her grace and goodness. She has been there for every moment. Up or down, thick or thin. She helped me write twenty books. I mean helped me. She listened as I read them aloud. No small sacrifice that. She also made corrections and creative and intelligent suggestions. Many of her ideas are in those books and in this one. We grew up together. Now we are growing old together.

This book is dedicated to her without whom my life would have been a wreck. Alison has been the most constant witness for God and the greatest proof of His grace in my life. This book is therefore dedicated to her who has loved me when I did not. We two have made this journey side-by-side, and she has given me joy.

To Alison

CONTENTS

FOREWORD

IN ALL MY years of ministry as well as in my travels all over the world, I have yet to meet someone as consequential to advancing the kingdom of God as Dr. Mark Rutland. He is truly a national treasure, and no one has done as much to advance the gospel and to disciple world-class leaders as Dr. Rutland. Whether helping to launch the careers of young pastors or identifying high-level executives, Dr. Mark has been a connector for hundreds of ministries and organizations.

For over fifteen years, Dr. Mark, as he's affectionally referred to at our campuses, has been a regularly scheduled speaker and the favorite guest speaker, and he's even served on our staff for several years as well. Recently, he has become a fixture at least twice a year for our senior luncheons, and he always leaves the seniors laughing and thinking about all that is possible with the time they have left. It came as no surprise to me that he would take the time to encourage and disciple senior citizens all over the world in his groundbreaking book *Keep On Keeping On*.

On the pages ahead you will discover powerful words of encouragement and instruction to the unsung heroes of every church—senior citizens. There is probably no speaker or teacher in the world who understands seniors today like Dr. Mark Rutland. Each chapter embodies years of experience working with the greatest generation and offers a practical plan and timely encouragement for the most unpredictable years of life.

So many times as people head into their latter years, there is the ever-present temptation to pull back and coast into the sunset. Dr. Rutland counters that thinking with a very practical yet powerful challenge to keep the pedal to the metal and leave a legacy. He embodies every single chapter of this book, and every page is filled with a much-needed word for seniors in the church today, providing timely guidance for those in their senior years of life. If you are fifty-five years or older, or are a leader who works with the seniors in your church or organization, this book will change the way you see life in the sunset years.

Over thirty years of pastoring the same church, I have witnessed the impact the seniors have had and continue to have in every area of church life. They lead small groups; they teach and sit on committees. They can be found serving all over our campuses every single Sunday. When we launch capital campaigns or collect special offerings for natural disasters, it's our seniors who have had the greatest impact and sacrifice through giving or volunteering.

We are all meant to live life to its fullest as long as we have breath. If you are reading this book, then you have proof that God is not done with you yet. I challenge you today to take time and read this book. You will discover that while we have no control over the aging process, we do have great control over the way we live our lives, the words we speak, and the attitude we carry into every task and interaction.

—JENTEZEN FRANKLIN
SENIOR PASTOR, FREE CHAPEL
NEW YORK TIMES BEST-SELLING AUTHOR

CHAPTER 1
KEEP ON KEEPING ON

*Do not go gentle into that good
night....Rage, rage against
the dying of the light.*
—DYLAN THOMAS

THERE IS A tree behind our house which, if it were to fall, would crush everything in its extensive fall zone. This massive oak, as sturdy as it is, as seemingly unlikely to topple over as it appears, poses an ever-present threat simply because it is there. Yet seldom, in fact almost never, do I think about the potential disaster inherent in its presence. The tree is there. That's all.

That is the issue with old age for most of our lives. From the moment we are born we begin to age and, for that matter, to die. Old age, with all its ravages, is our inevitable calamity, the tree in the yard; yet we do not obsess over it. We cannot live that way. We live in its lengthening shade and ignore, or try to ignore, the looming lethal possibility. That thing which has beset the elderly widow down the street, that which has so obviously hijacked her younger self, if ever she had one, that dreadful thing will never fall on us. Never. We are exempt.

We live our lives in a multiplicity of self-granted exemptions. It, whatever *it* is, will never happen to us. We drive past car crashes on the freeways of life, and we know the wrecked cars and the wrecked bodies we can see looked very like ours split seconds before the disaster. We do not drive on in unbearable dread that the same catastrophe will meet us just ahead. Crashes and deaths and tragedies happen, but we are exempt because, well, because we have decided we are.

The young still live in the frail and fleeting deception of a self-granted exemption about age. The young are bullet proof. They not only think they will live forever. They think they will live forever young. They will not age as we have done. They may not age at all, or if they do it will somehow be different for them. For us, their elders, the exemption has already proved to be a hopeless myth. We live in a world full of mirrors, and the face that stares back at us is ours. Our first reaction is, that cannot be me. And yet it is, and I am a shocking reality to myself.

Therein lies the great advantage of age over youth. We can remember being their age and how wonderful it felt to be exempt. They, on the other hand, do not believe old age will befall them, and they cannot imagine it. In fact, they do not dare imagine it. They are exempt. Even if they could envision such a future, God's grace would shield it from their inner eyes. If the average teenager got even a glimpse of himself at eighty, the nightmare would prove too much for him. That is why the young often seem so angry at the elderly. We scare the living daylights out of them. The very thought, the very hint of a thought—no, no, it is too horrible to contemplate. The exemption is real, they think. I am certain it is. I know it is.

Likewise, that is why the young make us so angry. They remind us of our own sweet delusion of which we have been so utterly despoiled. We see in them all our lost yesterdays, and it makes us want to shake them and scream, Don't you see what you're doing? You dumb little twit: You're wasting it!

So we stare or rather glare at each other across a fixed and uncrossable gulf. We cannot go back to where they are, and by the time they get to where we are, we will have gone, well, elsewhere.

In public speaking hardly anything delights me quite so much as to pick out some slim, attractive young married couple and speak directly to them in front of the entire audience.

"How old are you?" I ask them.

"Twenty-eight," he answers as if this is a perfectly reasonable age to be. "Twenty-six," she chirps merrily, oblivious to the humiliation I am about to inflict on them both.

"Look up here, son," I tell him. "Look at me. I am your future. As you are, so once was I. As I am, you soon will be." Delighting myself now in his half-hearted, embarrassed, and slightly frightened laughter, I drive the dagger deeper. "If you live long enough, someday you will look like *me*! Go on—take hold of the hair at your hairline and wiggle it back and forth. Now say, 'Bye-bye!'

"And, you, young lady, do me a favor. Run your finger over your upper lip. Isn't that soft? Haven't you figured it out? The hair that falls out of his head will grow on *your lip*!"

The crowd's roar of laughter, especially raucous amidst those over fifty, is a joy to any public speaker, exceeded only by the delicious look of horror on the young bride's face. After a moment the young couple themselves also laugh, or rather, they chuckle a bit self-consciously. Then I see it. I see them shake it off. I can actually see them shrug their slim young shoulders and smile reassuringly at each other. Their eyes twinkle in a silent and private message of hope. Ha ha. He's only kidding. How droll. A dash of humor in the lecture. Ha ha. What a funny little joke he played on us. The split second of reality rolls off them like spilt spaghetti off a plastic seat cover, and their exemption clicks back in place.

This book will be of no use to them. None whatsoever. At least not now. No mere book can penetrate the iron curtain of a self-granted exemption.

This book is for those who have stepped out from behind that impenetrable veil of comforting delusion into a new reality—which is not new and is not suddenly real. It was never not real. Age, like the tree in our yard, was always there and always ignored. We were sure it would never fall on us. Now that it has, we have to deal with it.

When everything, literally everything, hurts at least some of the time; when menus are all faintly printed in a blurred font distinguishable only in blazing light; when every trip to the grocery store is a challenging adventure that ends in the realization that we forgot at least three items which we also forgot to write on the list, which we left at home, so that we would not forget them; when such is our daily lot, we can no longer live in the precious delusion. We are what we never thought we would be.

This book is not for the young. Do not let them read it. They cannot bear it. This book is for those who now see that the good night is just around the bend. This book is for those who know the dying of the light is not a poignant literary device invented by some long-ago Welsh poet. It is their day-to-day reality. They have stumbled, quite literally, onto the truth. They are not, nor were they ever, exempt. They were merely deluded, and the loss of that beloved delusion is a severe dose of reality.

What shall we say then? Shall we indeed rage against the dying of the light? What good would it do? Some who think they are raging against the dying of the light are merely angry at their doctor because he is the age of their grandchildren and cannot make all the pain go away. No longer in possession of a self-granted delusion, they assume, in its place, a self-granted permission to rage, not at the dying of the light, but at the loud and careless youths who are not arthritic and whose temporary happiness is unbearably irritating. A man in his seventies thinks he is raging at the dying of the light when he screams at the kid next door for daring to chase his errant baseball into the yard. He fancies himself an eccentric rebel, a curmudgeonly James Dean; but he is actually an overgrown version of Kevin's big brother in *Home Alone*.

A waspish sixty-something businesswoman berates and humiliates her young male assistant. She thinks she is a strong leader, a woman undaunted by age and transcending gender. She thinks she is Ruth Ginsburg raging against the glass ceiling through which she views the dying of the light, but she is just a petty devil with no Prada to her name.

Living the last years of our lives as angry, aging tyrants is hardly what Dylan Thomas meant. The mere children who work at the ATT store trying to fix your phone, as if that were possible, as irritating and condescending as they may be, are not themselves the dying of the light. Raging against them is not a glorious refusal to go gentle into that good night. It is just ugly, undisciplined, and self-indulgent.

It is all just so confusing. Toys and tools that were common and needed are no longer even recognized. I saw a photo challenge on the internet, on the social media platform X to be precise. "Can you recognize this and what it was used for?" It was not a colonial era shingle froe. It was a photo of the manual crank for a car window! I suddenly realized that something I had used most of my life was now an antique, a quaint old thing, obsolete and unrecognizable to today's young people, who have never seen a car without powered windows.

It is in just such moments that one my age realizes I also am a quaint old thing, an antique, if not unrecognizable, at least largely invisible to the young. Their eyes are trained to see their own kind, not members of the tribe of the ancient mariner. Invisibility challenges one's pride and sense of significance. To be despised is one thing. To be overlooked, simply unseen, is quite another thing altogether. Having once been an actor one finds it surprising, to say the least, to be, at the end of the play, a part of the scenery.

Elwood P. Dowd, friend and companion to the invisible, six-foot rabbit Harvey, said, "In this world, you must be oh so smart or oh so pleasant. Well, for years, I was smart. I recommend pleasant."[1]

To paraphrase, "For years I was both young and visible. I recommend pleasant, even if invisible."

One must come to grips with the reality that the old person in the mirror is an antique, invisible and incomprehensible to the swarms of teenagers in the mall. The great thing is, having done that, life assumes an unstressed quality that is quite a relief after years of trying to be oh so smart, oh so youthful, and oh so seen. Pleasant invisibility is oh so much pleasanter.

This book is not about sounding retreat. It is about finding the joy in life as it is and not grieving about life as it was, or at least as I remember it. This book is about looking in the mirror and saying to the graying visage there, "You are no longer young. What a relief. Enjoy being pleasant and invisible."

Who am I, you may well ask, to be giving advice about aging well? My credentials are not on my resume. This is not a book by a geriatric psychologist, if such a thing even exists. My only recommendation is my own age, which at the time of this writing happens to be seventy-six. No barefoot boy am I. No beardless youth, regardless of his education or talent or "experience," so called, can write such a book as this. What experience could a mere child in his fifties have that would make him able to write a book on this topic? I sneer at such a notion. No callow youth in his sixties could or should undertake it, nor should they be listened to.

Seventy-six? Well, now you're talking. That and that alone makes me an expert. If you have ever known very many septuagenarians, you know we tend to be experts on a wide variety of topics and prepared to demonstrate said expertise at the drop of a hat. A male in his seventies is ready, at a moment's notice, to lecture on topics ranging from Native American folklore to the mating habits of Eurasian migratory birds. Which is one reason we, as a tribe, find ourselves frequently un-thronged. Solitary experts, but experts nonetheless. My credentials are seventy-six in number and growing annually.

You may have found this book in a used bookstore in the late 2070s. First, in this old book you have made a rare and wonderful discovery. I congratulate you on your biblio-archeological skill. Beyond that, I assure you that my expertise in the field addressed in this book, and in quite a few other fields too many to mention here, grew annually and exponentially right up to the moment of my death, which, I am certain, was tragic and the news of which was received by multitudes in a state of virtual despair.

A friend told me that one night as he exited an NBA game in Atlanta and made his way through a nearby parking garage, he was confronted by a man demanding ten dollars. At first my friend thought he was being mugged. Then he realized the man was a harmless but a bit overly aggressive panhandler.

"Look," my friend said to the beggar. "I happen to be an expert in my field, and my field happens to be marketing. You're going about this all wrong. You scared me, and frightened people are not generous people. I thought you were going to rob me. First of all, you can't just pop out of the darkness like that and demand ten bucks. Get over in the light. Clean up the setting a bit. Get rid of some of this trash.

"Second, inform the potential donor what your need is. Concisely explain the situation in your life. People just want to know the real human need.

"Third, don't demand the whole amount. Ask them to just make a dent in it. Ask them for fifty cents. That's nothing to most folks. Almost anyone will give you fifty cents. In twenty appeals the ten will be yours. You keep abruptly demanding ten dollars in a dark and dirty corner, you'll be out here all night."

My friend said that beggar drew himself to his full height and gathered his tattered overcoat about him and archly replied, "Look, fella. You don't have to give me the money if you don't want to, but don't tell me how to run my business."

I desire to tell no one how to run their business. Well, that is not true. In fact, like most people, especially male septuagenarians, I would like to tell many people how to run their businesses. Furthermore, whether or not they know it, many of them, especially government bureaucrats and convenience store employees, *need* me to tell them how to run their businesses.

What I do hope for in this book is to inspire a rebellion, to rally the great gray army and awaken its latent RQ (rebellion quotient for the uninitiated). We must rebel. We must do what Dylan Thomas said and rage against the dying of the light. The question is, How then shall we rage?

I suggest we dance and laugh. I beg your pardon. Did you say laughter and dancing? I did.

❧

Zorba the Greek is the story of a timid and inhibited English writer named Basil who goes to a Greek island to open a small lignite mine. On the boat over he is befriended—overwhelmed might be a better word—by Zorba, an exuberant, energetic peasant. Their stormy relationship finally explodes, literally, when Zorba designs a complicated system to get structural timbers for the mine from a nearby hillside owned by an orthodox monastery. A huge party is planned to celebrate its success; but instead it is a complete disaster. Everything is destroyed, and all those who came to celebrate with Zorba and Basil run for their lives.

The two men, Zorba, the irrepressible Greek, and Basil, the uptight and now defeated Englishman, sit alone amidst the wreckage eating the lamb prepared for the party. In the wake of this bitter disappointment, the end of the mine and the end of Basil's adventure in Greece, Basil makes a final and surprising request of his Greek friend.

He says, "Teach me to dance."

Zorba leaps to his feet laughing and immediately begins to teach Basil the sirtaki, a Greek folk dance. The movie ends with the two of them dancing at the scene of the mining/lumbering failure.

Dancing is a kind of rebellion against despair and defeat. Dancing says, I may be down but I'm not out. I will rise, and to the music in my mind I will dance with abandon.

Laughter in the face of life's most dismal moments is a form of resistance. Failure and pain and disappointment can be crushing. They can block the light and break the spine of our joy. We dare not let them win. We can become bitter and angry. We can march zombie-like into the fading light of our abandoned hopes.

There is another way.

Instead of ranting and whining and making ourselves and everyone around us miserable, what if we danced? What if we had a good belly laugh out of the whole crazy thing? Instead of bowing our heads and accepting defeat and failure as our inevitable destiny, what if we started laughing and danced? We need not go gentle into that good night. We needn't acquiesce. But what is our alternative? What if, in the fading light, we learned to laugh again, to laugh at life and death and age, and above all things at ourselves? We can fall on our knees and shake our fists at our broken dreams and ruined schemes and spoiled delusional exemptions. Or like Basil and Zorba we can laugh at shattered dreams and dance in rebellion at the blows of life that hoped to beat us down. To rise from defeat and dance is a mad, wonderful kind of rebellion. Laughter is joyful rage, an insurrection against the dying of the light. Yes. What if we could laugh again and dance in the dying of the light? What might that look like?

Remember sock hops? High school dances held in the gyms so everyone had to take their shoes off? Or did you call them record hops? Remember Danny and the Juniors? The Everly Brothers? Nobody at a dance is hankering for the past. They are just having fun where they are. As we age we become more and more aware of the tree in the yard. It could fall at any minute. What if I have a stroke? Am I becoming more forgetful? Is it something serious? How much longer will I enjoy good health?

Here's the thing. So what? I mean it. So what? It was always there. We begin to age and, in fact, to die the minute we are born. We know that. Deep inside we know it, but denial is a sweet elixir. The tree will never fall on me. What age does is a grand liberation, a deliverance from youth's idiotic, unreasonable faith in our own self-granted exemptions. What age does is not a bad thing. It is, however, a real thing. The aches and pains and surgeries, all the hammer blows upon this mortal coil, are reminders of our humanity and the reality that sooner or later the tree in the backyard always falls. Always. On everybody. No exceptions and no exemptions.

You're reading this. That means the tree in the backyard is still there, isn't it? It has not fallen on you. Not yet. How should we live knowing we live in its shadow? Let's be honest. Some stuff hurts that never hurt before. Some parts have already been replaced, and some others are not working all that great. Surgeries major and minor have been done or loom on the horizon. All these remind us of the tree in the yard. What then? We can live like frightened children staring up at its branches waiting for the crash. Or we can dance in its shade. We can laugh and enjoy today, this very day as it is and not as we wish it were. We can rebel! That's what we can do.

A friend, a football-loving woman of the South, a Georgia Bulldog fan through and through, made an important comment about old age. She called it "life in the red zone." Southern girls know their football. For the uninformed, the red zone is that portion of an American football field between the twenty-yard line and the goal line. Her analogy is apt. By our senior years we have finally made our way up the field however easily or despite agonizing battles for every yard. Either way, now the goal line is in view.

Once in the red zone, the expectation for teams to score goes way up. That's where they prove who they really are. So it is with us. The goal line is in view. We can flounder around in embarrassing futility, or we can make these last few yards what they should be. I do not want to stall out in the red zone. I want to finish it right. I do not want to rest in the red zone. I have fought my way up the field. In the red zone I want to press on with my eyes fixed on the goal line, and at the end I want to dance in the end zone. That's called keeping on keeping on.

I wonder how many seniors' ministries in how many churches are called the "Young at Heart Club." All too often that is just a trite name not at all indicative of the mentality of its members.

Juan Manuel Cascales was born in 1911 in Mexico but immigrated to the United States with his mother as an eight-year-old boy. He became a well-known musician, arranger, and composer who used the name Johnny Richards. Not the least of his credits is a song he wrote for Frank Sinatra, "Young at Heart," in which he references surviving to 105.[2] Richards himself did not survive to a hundred and five or even to sixty. Sadly, he died of a brain tumor at the age of fifty-six.

Francis Albert Sinatra, however, is the far more famous of the two, and it is his name that is associated with "Young at Heart." Old Blue Eyes may have been wrong about many things, among which were Ava Gardner, well, actually marriage in general, and loose associations with the Mafia. One thing he and Richards were right about is in the lyrics: To be young at heart is the best part. It is the sublime revolt.

To be young at heart is the best part. It is also the sublime revolt, the sweet rage against the dying of the light. How do we live in the fall zone of that ominous tree in the yard? We keep on. We keep on laughing and playing and dancing. We keep on being gracious and loving and kind. We keep on being generous. We keep giving and doing and going. In short we just refuse to quit being young at heart. We keep on being jolly and forgiving. We keep on dreaming and giving.

Frank Sinatra a bit too far back for you? OK. How about the Gentrys? I *know* you remember the Gentrys and "Keep on Dancing." The lyrics were so simple and repetitive they must have been written in a matter of minutes. I bet you cannot recall five words beyond the ones that tell us to keep dancing and prancing.

I know you remember when the song just stops dead silent right in the middle only to be kicked back on by that fabulous snare drum fill. You say you cannot dance and you're too old to prance? Of course. All this talk of dancing is a metaphor for a joyful, celebratory life right to the end. Sinatra was right. Be young at heart. The Gentrys were also right. Keep on.

The tree is there. Oh yeah, the tree is there all right. But it hasn't fallen on me yet, and until it does I for one intend to keep on keeping on.

CHAPTER 2

KEEP ON LAUGHING

Laugh, and the world laughs
   with you;
Weep, and you weep alone;
For the sad old earth must
   borrow its mirth,
But has trouble enough of its
   own.

—ELLA WHEELER WILCOX

SHAKESPEARE WROTE THAT life "is a tale told by an idiot, full of sound and fury, signifying nothing."[1]

Shakespeare had it wrong. Life is not so much told by an idiot as it is all about idiots, and I am not the least of them. Idiots, not all of whom are in Washington, lack the creativity to make up such a tale as a life is, any life, including mine. The randomness, the wild lurches to port and back to starboard in the midst of heavy seas, the deserts and the deluges back-to-back and back again make

19

me know that God is real. He must be. God is not the Divine Idiot writing our lives as some meaningless yarn full of sound and fury and utterly lacking significance. He does not dictate every detail. We, all of us humans, have added plenty of both sound and fury into our own lives and into the lives of others. What a comedy!

Here is the point. Only God could take the whole mad, random mess and weave it all together into a lovely quilt. In my life, for example, though I am not sure of what it is an example, there has been plenty of sound and fury, far too much of both. Of sadness, my own and the sadnesses I have caused, there has been no lack. I have made no secret of my battle, especially in my earlier years, with dark depression. The thing that kept me sane, at least as sane as I have been, is that I never took myself very seriously. I could always, well, usually, see what was funny about it all, and about me in particular. Despite the moments of pain and the seasons of grief, both of which I have experienced, I have also had more than my share of laughter.

Proverbs 17:22 says, "A merry heart does good like a medicine" (MEV).

I determined early on to take my medicine like a big boy. A merry heart may come more naturally to some than others. Circumstances may make for more or less merriment, to be sure, but the bottom line is we can choose to be merry. If there is one thing that can make our senior years better and healthier it is the sweet, sweet medicine of laughter. My advice to seniors is simple: Laugh lots.

For me there has always been plenty to laugh about. I have spent a great deal of my life in church, and the funniest stuff happens in church. The church crowd is not always eager to acknowledge the humor, and I find that level of denial quite impressive. I think a new question should be added to ordination interviews: Do you see what is funny about us? Any potential ordinand who cannot answer in the affirmative, enthusiastically and with anecdotal evidence, should be summarily rejected. I have preached in churches on every inhabited continent of the globe. Some are more willing to laugh than others, but precious few see the humor in themselves.

One brutal winter I preached in several churches in different parts of Norway. Not perhaps the jolliest churches in the world, but they knew humor when they heard it. It's just that their response was to acknowledge it afterward rather than to actually laugh at it. They would often just stare back intensely while I preached and later say, "That was really funny."

As an American I would have much preferred outright laughter in the moment. At least a chuckle.

What I got was a stiff, frozen stiff perhaps, compliment later in the parking lot. A sincere handshake and a compliment without so much as a smile. "That joke you told in there was really funny." I decided the delayed response was a result of the frigid weather. I have never preached in Antarctica. If there is a church somewhere in that frozen terrain, I leave it to others heartier than I.

As a thoroughgoing Pentecostal, I am unapologetic in my convictions that the gifts, the signs and wonders, and the miracles, indeed all the manifestations of the Holy Spirit, are still operational in the contemporary church. How could anything else be true? Was Don McLean correct? Did the Holy Ghost catch the last train for the coast? Of course not. Furthermore, there is nothing funny about the Holy Spirit. I am not irreverent, although some see me as such. While there is nothing funny about the Spirit of God Himself, there is plenty funny about the people of God.

One Pentecostal pastor told me he invited an evangelist to preach in his church to the displeasure of a certain woman, a member of the church, who was a self-proclaimed prophetess. We on our side of the aisle, that being the Pentecostal/charismatic side, feel badly for traditional churches bereft of such prophetesses. Indeed we would gladly share some of ours. They and they alone can hear from God. They alone have the red phone to heaven.

This particular prophetess, being no exception, informed the pastor that God did not want that evangelist to come. The pastor said exactly what he should have, that he was the pastor and that until God spoke to him otherwise, the evangelist was coming. He advised the sister that she did not have to approve or even come to the services, but the evangelist was coming. She would not leave well enough alone. They never do.

The first night of the revival, just as the guest began to preach, the woman sprang into action. Stepping out into the center aisle, she pointed her finger in the evangelist's face and began to shout with just the correct prophetic ululation in her voice.

"Thus saith the Lord! Thou thinkest that thou art a humdinger!" she wailed. "But thou art not a humdinger, saith the Lord. Thou art a dinger!"

The pastor told me he froze at the controls. Nothing in life or leadership had prepared him for that moment, and he was paralyzed. It was the evangelist who saved the day. He stared at the woman briefly, then burst out laughing. Not chuckling. Laughing. A thunderous explosion of laughter, which was immediately followed by laughter all across the auditorium. Laughter in a church feeds itself. Soon the entire church was laughing to the point of tears.

This was too much for the prophetess. Her Bible under her arm, she charged toward the exit, under which she paused only briefly. Raising her arm dramatically, she bellowed, "I'll never darken the doors of this church again."

The pastor said it was the hour of deliverance.

The only emotionally mature, psychologically balanced, and spiritually authentic response for some things is a good belly laugh. Some things in life are funny. Some things about you are funny. We can all see them. Look in the mirror and get in on the joke.

The amazing part of this story, however, is that that mean-spirited, self-glorifying, false prophetess was right about one thing. She was right about the evangelist. Indeed, she was right about all of us. We spend so much of our lives, of our emotional and spiritual energy, trying to convince each other, God, and ourselves that we are humdingers. It's a losing battle, but we fight on.

Here's the sad part or the funny part or the both-at-the-same-time part. No one believes it anyway. We all know, deep down inside, that we are dingers. We have merely entered into a mutually agreed upon covenant of suspended disbelief.

The story is told of a young man who took a seat at a bus stop and found himself on the bench, all alone with a nun. He regarded her for a moment, dressed as she was, in her classical black-and-white habit.

"Sister," he said, "I wouldn't offend you for anything, but I must tell you something. I have always harbored a secret desire to one day kiss a nun. I don't know where this came from, but I feel before I die I must fulfill this wish. Please let me kiss you. Nothing passionate. Just a peck on the cheek. No one can see us. What would it hurt?"

The sister studied the young man a moment and decided he seemed harmless enough. "All right," the nun said. "I cannot imagine what it could hurt. OK. I'll let you kiss me on two conditions. You have to be single, and you must be a Catholic."

"Wow!" he said. "This is my day! I am single, and I happen to be a Catholic."

With that he leaned over and gently kissed her cheek. Then he laughed in her face. "The joke's on you, Sister. I'm married, and I'm a Baptist!"

"No," said the nun. "The joke's on you. My name is Kevin, and I'm on my way to a costume party."

Absent an authentic sense of humor, we turn life into a pathetic costume party pretending to believe each other's rented outfits. That is one thing that is so sad about the so-called "cancel culture."

Nothing, least of all us, is funny anymore. Ever hear the phrase "deadly serious"? How about this one? "Serious as a heart attack." A life without laughter is deadly indeed, and a heart attack may just be what such joylessness leads to.

Many years ago a fellow minister lost his arm in a terrible accident. I went to the hospital hoping to comfort him following this awful amputation. "Don't worry," he said. "All things work together for good....I'm not a great preacher. I could never have hoped to be the best preacher in the state. But I may very well become the best one-armed preacher in the state. Who knows? Maybe in the nation."

Perspective is everything.

Life is important. All life. From conception to heaven, life is precious and unspeakably important to God. Therefore it goes without saying that life should be important to us as well. It does not, however, actually go without saying. It gets said and said and said. We hear it all the time. This or that life matters. Your life matters. You are important to God. And all of that is true. It's just that we draw the unfortunate conclusion that because our lives are important to God, whatever is important to me must therefore be of ultimate importance to God and to the universe or, if it is not, it should be. We turn pro-life into pro-me. Our egos take hold of one end of a great truth and bolt up the blind alley of self-importance until the *truth* part is blurred beyond recognition and the remaining *self* part is in neon lights.

Self-importance, self-exaltation, self-everything, indeed all the hyphenated sins, destroy all of humility and meekness and at last humor. The thugs of antifa and the white-robed wizards of the KKK have far more in common than either of them wants to believe. Rip away their bedsheets and their balaclavas and they are the same angry, self-important little fascists. If there is one thing fascists hate it is humor, especially at their expense.

I don't suppose anyone really enjoys being the butt of a joke, but a fascist will kill you for it. Or fire you or demote you or cancel you or whatever he can. There is something hysterically funny about a grown man with a bedsheet over his head. Angry protesters screaming nonsensical slogans, literally nonsensical, are just plain laughable. Sad, yes. More than a bit scary, yes. But above all, funny. They have become so important in their own minds that whatever they are saying or rather screaming becomes so important that they wind up saying some really funny stuff. Their wild-eyed hysterics are actually funny. Their crazed eyes become the google-eye spectacles we used to wear at Halloween. They see nothing, absolutely nothing, funny in anything they do, which is, of course, the funniest thing of all since a great deal of what they do couldn't be made up by the Coen brothers.

Oh, if only the trap of humorless self-importance were confined to LGBTQ protesters and retired generals. Alas, the church is rife with it. Preachers can become so convinced of their own importance that as far as they are concerned their every word is an apple of gold in a silver bowl. Who dares challenge the man of God?

Intoxicated with the wildly exaggerated importance of serving on the board of a local church or college, laymen can actually begin to think they and their opinions are of wildly exaggerated importance. Absurd inconsequentialities become a no man's land of meetings in the back room of a church no one ever heard of or a college that imagines itself to be infinitely significant. Board members looking for all the world like Twiddle Dee and Tweedle Dum in a cage match live in some fantasy world where what they say is important and must be heard and heeded. Humorless self-importance turns leadership, especially church leadership, into the theater of the absurd. No. It isn't even good theater of the absurd. It turns it into absurd theater of the absurd.

❧

It is said one never forgets one's first time. My first funeral, that is, was incredibly unforgettable. In fact it was a life-changing gift of God. That I was the lead pastor of a Methodist church at twenty-two is a bit absurd itself. Be that as it may, I was fishing friends with one man, Clyde, who attended quite regularly, whenever he was sober, that is. Demon rum was, in fact, Clyde's demon, and when it had hold of him it was awful. When he sobered up, however, Clyde was repentant, generous, and, best of all, deeply humble. He also had a remarkable sense of humor and kept me in stitches on every fishing trip.

Clyde was a true unicorn, a man of the soil, an uneducated farmhand who loved his tribe but saw what was funny about them. He had a genuine Southern rural sense of humor that, could he have stayed sober long enough at a stretch, might easily have made him a success in comedy. He was that rare breed who could laugh at those who, like him, were mostly uneducated, but his humor was never cruel or mean-spirited.

His wife, Emma, was not thus gifted. Virtually everything Emma said was mean-spirited. She was one of the bitterest, sourest women I've ever had the misfortune to meet. I do not blame all this on Emma. I'm sure life with Clyde was no bowl of cherries. It's just that for me, over the short haul, Clyde made me laugh and Emma made me want to join the French Foreign Legion. She was not a Methodist as I was at that time, but a Primitive Baptist, a denomination sometimes called Hardshell Baptists. Emma's shell was a bit harder than most. Her husband's friendship with me, or more precisely mine with him, was a mystery to Emma. Why would a preacher, even a Methodist, want to be friends with, or even be seen with, the likes of Clyde? It was beyond her.

When Clyde passed away, Emma insisted on two things. One was that I preach part of the funeral. The other was that it be held in her Primitive Baptist church, which Clyde had steadfastly refused to enter. I think she was determined that Clyde attend her church one time whether he liked it or not and that he would be at the altar. Or perhaps she hoped against hope that one's port of embarkation might make a difference in one's destination. As to my preaching at the funeral, who knows? A nod to Clyde's wishes perhaps. Regardless of why, she insisted upon it. I tried to be let off, assuring her it made no difference to Clyde, but she was intractable.

I drove to the funeral, my first funeral, in a nervous sweat. Emma's Hardshell Baptist church was well back in the hills, and I knew intuitively that I would be out of place. The sight of the church did nothing to dispel my darkest fears. It was a tiny, dilapidated, and screen-less caricature, a movie set for a film about religious hillbillies, in which movie I was doomed to play the outsider, the unwanted citified preacher.

Beside the church sprawled the ancient cemetery in which stood a solitary tent advertising the funeral home and shielding Clyde's freshly dug grave from the drizzle. It had rained hard the night before, and the slate gray skies still dripping half-heartedly only added to my gloom.

The elderly pastor paced impatiently in the side yard like the minatory relic he was. He ignored my extended hand and scowled at me over his wire-rimmed bifocals in naked distaste.

"Are you the Methodist preacher?" he asked, but when he said "Methodist," it sounded rather like *mass murderer.*

"I am."

"Well, I did not want you here," he snarled.

"Sir," I said, "we may not agree on anything else all day, but we agree on that. I did not want to be a part of this either."

"The 'widder' wanted you. That's the only reason you're here."

"Exactly," I agreed. "Let's just try to minister to the 'widder' and get this over with, and I will hit the road."

"Do you want to go first or second?" he demanded, and for a moment I could not think what he meant until it finally dawned on me that he meant the speaking order in the service.

"Sir, it's your church. You decide."

"No!" He was nearly shouting by this time. "Answer me. First or second?"

"All right," I said, "second."

"No! You go first."

It all went downhill from there. Nothing I did or said was right, and, of course, since it was my first funeral it may very well have been wrong. The *piece de resistance* was my brief sermon. I shared about my friendship with Clyde, that I liked him and that he was, despite his weaknesses, a kind and generous man. I said that he would give a friend in need the shirt off his back. I saw people in the congregation nod their heads in obvious agreement, and I was encouraged.

Finally I spoke about Clyde's infectious sense of humor. I recalled how on one of our fishing trips Clyde had somehow incredibly gotten a fishhook in his own ear and that despite his pain he couldn't stop laughing. Everyone in the room knew Clyde, and they chuckled at the image, which they found not at all hard to believe. I then had a prayer thanking God for His unfailing grace in the face of our many weaknesses. Several soft but genuine-sounding amens indicated approval, if not for the sentiments at least for my brevity. I sat down feeling that for my first time up to bat, I may not have homered but I had hit a good solid single.

The old pastor rose to differ. He lambasted me in a febrile rant so overheated I thought, and actually fantasized, he might have a cerebral hemorrhage. No such luck. He denounced "irreverent young preachers who tell jokes at funerals." He went on to announce God's disgust, not disapproval, *disgust*, with preachers who did so. I was mortified. Like the poor souls in Luke 23, I longed for the mountains to cover me.

At last it was over. As the pallbearers came forward and hefted the casket, the old preacher and I left the platform and led them and the congregation out to the waiting grave. As we walked I recovered myself enough to ask if he wanted me to have any part at the graveside service.

"No! You've done enough."

I was immensely relieved. I wanted nothing but to endure whatever polemical diatribe he chose to deliver at the grave, jump in my car, and head for civilization. I certainly did not intend to force my way into any extension of a funeral I wanted no part of from the very start. The ancient Baptist preacher was certain I would try to insinuate myself, however, and he intended to personally obstruct any such invasion. As the pallbearers carefully placed Clyde's casket on the sling, the old preacher stepped out to the very edge of the AstroTurf at the head of the casket in a dramatic, preemptive attempt to thwart any sly move I might make at blockade running.

When he did, he stepped out too far and shot down into the grave. Clyde's casket, a bit loose on the sling, obliged his entry, and the preacher plunged into the wet grave up to his chest. At that point the casket swung back in against him, and Clyde had that preacher penned like a bug on an insect collection.

"Get me out! Get me out!"

His frantic screams were music to my ears. Vengeance is mine, saith the Lord! He was wedged so tightly that finally the grave diggers, who had gone to their truck for a smoke, had to be retrieved to crank the casket up. Several men tugged the preacher out while he flailed and hissed at them like a captured snake. What he blamed them for I cannot imagine.

The old preacher was coated in rain-clotted red Georgia clay from his armpits to his feet. His suit was without a doubt beyond reclamation. His shoes were no better off. Shocked Primitive Baptist saints stared in unbelief at the specter standing before them dripping globs of wet clay and snarling at anyone who tried to help him, especially his poor wife, who dabbed at him in utter futility with a lace hanky.

Just at that moment my eyes met those of "the widder." It was as though I could hear what Emma was thinking. Clyde would love this. Until that moment I had never heard Emma laugh. I doubted she possessed the capacity. She suddenly proved me wrong. She did not so much laugh as she erupted. When she did, the Hardshell dam in that little cemetery broke open and out poured a tidal wave of pent-up Baptist laughter. The old preacher stormed off to his car, his wife mincing along behind him; but in the cemetery, laughter poured down like latter rain.

In that little cemetery I heard the voice of Wisdom. It said two things I have never forgotten. The first was simple. At a graveside service stand back from the grave. The second was more nuanced. If you fall in, laugh first.

A sense of humor is not knowing what's funny. It's knowing what is funny about you. Anger and self-pity leave little room for laughter, and laughter is the social witness of a merry heart.

Age and all its aches and pains rot the sweet fruit of merriment on the vine and fertilize the bitter weeds of self-pity. The older we get the more important it is to laugh, especially at ourselves. All the things about age that we used to laugh at are still funny. It's just that now we do them. Remember the old man routine that Tim Conway used to perform on *The Carol Burnett Show*? Remember how he would shuffle his feet and lose his place in conversations? Remember when he washed his hands in the fish bowl? Oh, how we laughed. Remember? It's still funny; only now it's *us*!

It is a sad life indeed that constantly rails at everyone, "It's not funny!"

Yes, whatever *it* is, is probably funny. When you spend a half hour looking all over the house for your reading glasses and find they were on your head the whole time, that's funny. When you are talking with younger folks and realize they have no idea, none whatsoever, what a pay phone is, that's funny. When you think there's still an idle screw on your car, that's funny. When you realize that to change the idle speed in your car requires that the computer in your car must celebrate Holy Communion with the computer at the dealership, you have to see that's funny.

My wife and I were at a dinner party when the movie *Bonnie and Clyde* was mentioned. A pathetically culturally deprived man in his mere forties had never heard of the movie, nor of Faye Dunaway. I patiently explained that it was a ground-breaking movie that had come out nearly sixty years earlier.

A man at the table who was about my age erupted.

"What are you saying?" he howled. "Not sixty years ago. That movie didn't come out sixty years ago."

"No?" I asked. "When do you think it came out?"

"I know exactly when it came out," he said. "It came out the year I graduated from high school: 1967."

"Right," I said as I counted them off on my fingers. "Seventy-seven, eighty-seven, ninety-seven, 2007, 2017, 2023…that's fifty-six years."

He looked gut punched. "Oh, no," he moaned. "You're right. Fifty-six years."

Now *that's* funny. You gotta admit it. At the horrified look on his face the whole table laughed. When we think something happened a "few years ago" and it turns out to be more than a half century, you've got to laugh. You'd better. There's nothing to do about it. Faye Dunaway is eighty-two! Warren Beatty is nearly ninety. Tempus has fugit-ed! And if you cannot laugh, avoid mirrors at all costs.

As Ella Wilcox said, "Laugh and the world laughs with you. Weep and you weep alone." No one wants to be in a hospital. No one wants to be sick or in pain. Growl at the nurse with a hypodermic in her hand and you may wish you'd laughed.

There is no season of life in which the ability to laugh at oneself is more important and, by the way, more winsome than the senior years. Lines come with age. There's no stopping them, but laugh lines are infinitely more beautiful than frown lines.

Years ago my mother and grandmother were having a celebratory birthday brunch at a ritzy hotel restaurant in Dallas. An unaccompanied elderly man came in and was seated at the very next table. They could not help overhearing his exchange with a querulous waitress. When he ordered two large glasses of tomato juice, she challenged him.

"The large glasses are quite large. I'll bring you one, and if you want another after it I'll bring it then."

"Look," the man said. "I know what I want. Bring me two large glasses of tomato juice. Bring them together."

"That's silly," she insisted. "Why in the world would you want two at the same time?"

"See here," the man said sternly. "You're not my mother."

"I know I'm not your mother, but that is just ridiculous and you know it. Why in the world do you want two at the same time?"

"Is it any of your business if I should drink one and pour one over my head?"

"No. But you're not going to do that, and you know it."

With that she retreated to the kitchen and returned with two huge glasses of tomato juice.

Depositing these on the stranger's table she stepped back, crossed her arms, and stood there looking for all the world like a hall monitor at an elementary school.

The customer chugged the first one without once removing the glass from his lips. Then without even looking at the waitress he calmly poured the second over his head. The juice like a lurid river of blood flowed over his hair, his white shirt, suit and tie, and down onto the tablecloth, from whence it began to drip onto the floor. With that he tossed a few dollars onto the table, thanked the stunned waitress, and left as the entire restaurant erupted in applause and laughter.

I have no idea who that well-dressed old gentleman was, but he knew the secret. The old guy with tomato juice on his head made the snarky young waitress in her starched uniform the butt of the joke. Laugh, or pour tomato juice over your head, and the world laughs with you. Snark and you snark alone.

CHAPTER 3

KEEP ON LETTING GO

*The funny thing about chasing
the past is that most people
wouldn't know what to do
with it if they caught it.*
—ATTICUS

LETTING GO IS among the most important of all the keys to aging gracefully. Yet, as important as it is, it sounds like a hollow platitude. I have heard it said a million times and seen it on bumper stickers and buttons: "Let Go and Let God." The challenge is making that truism real in real time and in real life. We are somehow predisposed to hold on to stuff, wounds no less than blessings. Some people are emotional hoarders. Their lives are stuffed with junk they should have sent to the dump years ago. The question is, What do we let go of? What do we hold on to? We often memorialize the wrong stuff and jettison that to which we should desperately cling. Some things need to go in the rubbish bin never to be retrieved. Other things need to be cherished and enjoyed like beloved heirlooms.

Exodus 17:14 is a fascinating verse. "And the Lord said unto Moses, Write this for a memorial in a book, and rehearse it in the ears of Joshua, for I will utterly put out the remembrance of Amalek from under heaven."

Why would God tell Moses to recount the wild, wonderful, dramatic story of the Exodus in Joshua's hearing? Joshua had been there for all of it. Because they both needed to share the memory. Moses needed to tell it, and Joshua needed to hear it again. Some memories need to be shared repeatedly. The Amalekites need to be forgotten. The trick is knowing which is which.

Some years ago I did some counseling with a man named Howard. He was a World War II vet in his eighties, and the sessions were strenuous for both of us, to say the least. The struggle was sorting through his war memories in an effort to find which were worth keeping and which needed to be jettisoned. Some of those memories were of camaraderie, of the men with whom he served and came to care about. They were good memories of courage and sacrifice and shared hardships. Those he needed to keep rehearsing just as the Lord told Moses to do.

Some of his memories, however, were horrific. Those memories were what I call "Amalekite memories." Those needed to be "put out of remembrance." Easier said than done. At first he just could not let them go. Or rather he felt deep inside that he should not let them go. Something had gotten all twisted around in his conscience. He felt he needed to be punished by remembering those things. Every session, every time we met, all we did was practice "letting go." Instead of clutching at the memory when it came to mind, he worked with me to let go, to release those memories to an area we called "the Amalekite land of non-remembrance." It was a discipline for him and not an easy one. But those WWII guys were tough, and Howard was one of the best.

One day he said to me, "I like following orders. It's how I was raised and trained and how I fought my way ashore on two islands. Are you ordering me to let go?"

"No, Howard, I am not ordering you, but it is nonetheless an order. It's just not my order. It's God's order. When those things come to mind, let go. From now on that's a standing order from heaven."

"Let go? That's it?"

"Yes. That's the order."

"And keep on letting go. Right?"

"Exactly. Let go. And keep on letting go."

That was Howard's turning point, and it can be a huge victory for anyone, especially in our senior years. So many memories have piled up like nasty dust bunnies under the bed. Let go! Where you were wrong, give the memory of those things to God and receive His grace. Where you were wronged, do exactly the same thing. Give those memories to God and receive His grace.

St. Paul had some bad memories. He could have let them haunt him, but he learned to let go of those memories that needed to be un-remembered.

"Forgetting those things which are behind, and reaching forth for those things which are before, I press toward the mark for the prize" (Phil. 3:13–14).

Some memories, Amalekite memories, need to go to the dump and stay there, but not every memory is of the Amalekite kind. Our sweetest memories are treasures of inestimable worth. Age can steal so much from us. The loss of our memories, not the loss of our memory, but the loss of specific memories is among the dearest of thefts. Clutch them, retell them, share them, and never let go of them. Rehearse them just as God ordered Moses to do.

The first United Methodist church I pastored was a small student appointment in rural North Georgia. That part of the country, north of Atlanta, has grown to be a gentrified suburb. I doubt if the yuppies who live there now have any idea of what it was like in 1971. I look back on those early salad years at a tiny country church as some of the most important and formative of my life. They were "Andy of Mayberry" years, and I cherish the memories.

There were sweet people in that church who loved Alison and me and overlooked our atrocious ignorance. We were both suburbanites barely into our twenties. Neither of us had ever lived on a farm or even worked in a garden. We grew up trading comic books and playing board games with kids in sprawling suburban neighborhoods. Rural Georgia was a culture shock to us. I am certain we were a shock to the members of that little church, most of whom had lived through the hardships of Depression-era farming. Among the members of that church were some of my life's most memorable characters, the very thought of whom makes me smile to this day.

One Saturday Alison and I were invited to pick beans in a woman's backyard garden. We had never picked vegetables except to pluck them, in their cans, from off grocery store shelves. That morning we took brown paper sacks and reported for duty, excited at the opportunity to gain a new experience. The garden was huge, covering most of her backyard, but, alas, as we walked the verdant rows we saw no beans. The lush green plants were there in architecturally straight lines, but no beans were on them. We did not know what to do. Should we tell the lady the bad news? What had caused it? Perhaps the beans had been stolen in the night. Finally we tapped on the back door and sheepishly informed the woman that her plants were in fact bean-less.

She stared at us with naked pity and marched wordlessly out to the garden where, pulling the plants back, she revealed the luxuriance suspended below. We picked a sack of beans and went home. She was discreet enough not to mention this pathetic incident ever again. Apparently she never even mentioned it to her husband, who still treated me with respect.

Among the most unique of the members was a confirmed bachelor named Harold who lived with his elderly mother in a large farmhouse on a hill across the road from the church. He was older than I and a bit of an odd duck, but we became fast friends. I was twenty-three, and I thought Harold was aging rapidly at the ripe old age of forty-one. Harold was a constant source of amazement to me, as I am sure I was to him. Even more important, he was a veritable goldmine of humorous sermon illustrations from which I extract usable nuggets to this day.

Harold loved fires. I mean, he *loved* fires. He was not a pyromaniac. I am certain he never set any house fires, but having said that, he took an exuberant delight in them. Harold attended house fires like a passionate Pentecostal attends revivals. If they were close enough to drive to, he went. He would stand by the roadside and watch the firefighters do their jobs, and he would study the poor families as they in turn watched their world go up in flames. He tried to interest me in this hobby, and I did, in fact, go with him to a couple of fires.

He would come screeching into our parsonage driveway, spraying gravel and madly honking his horn. The moment I appeared in the doorway Harold would shout hysterically, "Come on, Preacher! There's a fire over on Sandy Plains Road. Let's go fast."

And he meant fast. He knew every back road, and he drove like a bat. As we approached we could see the dreadful glow against the night sky. He would park as close to the action as possible, and we would jog the rest of the way. We watched in silence. It turns out one does not talk at fires. Who knew? Afterward he would talk, recounting various aspects of the fire with amazing memory for the details. But while the fire raged he remained in rapt silence, speaking only rarely and never taking his eyes off the fire. In a hushed and reverential tone, Harold would whisper some tidbit of information he thought might help a nonfire-going flatlander such as I.

"The roof is just about to go." His soft but awe-struck utterances were the theatrical whisper of dark Shakespearean tragedy. Beneath Harold's thick Southern accent, I heard a hint of Laurence Olivier.

Indeed, Harold seemed inclined to drama. I, being barely out of my teens, kept hours those country folks could not understand. In front of the church was a sign with a lockable glass door behind which were moveable metal letters and numbers. It was among my duties to change the sign as needed. My incredibly intriguing sermon titles were announced on this sign each Monday. One Sunday night I went up to the church about 11 p.m. Being young and having no cows to milk the next morning, I felt this was a perfectly reasonable time to change the church sign. Not so Harold.

I saw the light appear on Harold's front porch high on the hill across the street only seconds before I heard the shotgun. The soft metallic rain of birdshot on the pavement between us was proof that Harold had me in his sights.

"Harold," I yelled, "don't shoot! It's me. It's the preacher."

"What are you doing down there?"

"I'm changing the church sign."

Long silence.

"It's eleven o'clock, Pastor."

"I know."

Porch light goes off. Silence. The incident was never mentioned by either of us ever again. I'm certain, absolutely certain, he did not want the rest of the church or the community to know something so bizarre as my late-night, sign-changing activities. That is the kind of gossip that can get a pastor in trouble. I, for my part, felt it indiscreet to mention his attempt to shotgun the pastor.

It was in part because of this same church sign that Harold learned and subsequently shared with me a great insight into prayer and the sovereign will of God. Following a rash of mailbox bashing in the area, Harold was afraid vandals would smash the glass in the church sign. This fear had obviously made him a bit trigger happy. It also made him determined to catch the vandals.

One night Harold awoke to laughter across the street, and he just knew it was the teenagers he wanted to catch in the very act of sign destruction. With his bedroom windows open he could hear their laughter and what he took to be beer cans hitting the church parking lot. Harold jumped out of bed and ran out to his carport. When his car started, the car in the church parking lot took off up the highway in the direction of Marietta, the closest town of any size. Screeching out of his own driveway, Harold was in hot pursuit in seconds.

Harold told me all about it the next day at church.

"I tell you, Pastor, I learned some stuff about prayer last night. God is so good He will answer prayers we pray in faith."

"Yes, Harold, that is certainly true," I said.

"But that ain't the half of His goodness. God is so good that no matter how much faith we have, God ain't gonna answer prayers that are bad for us."

"Why, yes," I said, "but what about last night...?"

"I'm trying to tell you. I chased them fellows for nearly twenty miles as fast as I could drive. The whole way I prayed that God would send a cop. If the police saw us going that fast I just knew they'd stop us both, and I could tell what they had been a doing. I just kept praying. Send a cop. Please, Lord, just send a cop. Just before we got to Highway 41, I happened to look down at myself and realized I was naked as a jaybird. I had been sleeping in the nude, and I got so excited to catch them fellows I forgot it. I slammed on the brakes and did a U-turn. I'm telling you, Pastor, I drove home mighty careful, and I was praying the whole way. Cancel that last prayer, Lord. Cancel that last prayer."

Theology in action is a powerful thing to behold.

The thing that the ministry can bludgeon out of a pastor is a love for people. People can be a shock to a naive young pastor. The one thing no one ever seems to teach in Bible schools and seminaries is that sheep bite. Some are man eaters. It really is horrible what some churches do to their pastors, what some boards do to wreck the joy and faith of ministers of the gospel. In fact, it is not always huge congregational blowups or vicious board meetings. More often it's just the lack of appreciation and all the petty remarks and thoughtless criticisms. It's death by a thousand cuts, and it can bleed the love out of a pastor.

Folks like Harold can restore a pastor's faith and rebuild his soul. I went through a vicious attack while pastoring at another church years later. It was hard on me, on Alison, and on our children. But all the venom poured out at that church cannot cancel out the genuine affection of folks like Harold. He was uneducated and unsophisticated. He pronounced taco as "tayco" and attended house fires with religious zeal; but he loved the Lord and he loved me and he made me laugh. These fifty years later when I think of Harold chasing those teenagers "as naked as a jaybird," it still makes me laugh. Besides that, his theology of prayer and the sovereignty of a good God were entirely correct.

Harold was hardly the only character in that church. The Hartsfield girls were not girls, and they were not sisters. They were mother and daughter, and they were unforgettable. Mrs. Hartsfield was a widow in her sixties. A large widow. She was a Tugboat Annie type with a monumental bosom under which she would cross her arms and occasionally hoist the entire operation skyward as she talked. It made for a very arresting visual punctuation. Furthermore she had developed the ability to let her false teeth drop loose then snap them back in place with a loud clack. The combined effect was remarkable.

Maybelle, her daughter, looked for all the world like Ruth Buzzi's character, Shakuntala, on *Rowan & Martin's Laugh-In*. I reference Shakuntala not only for those who can remember her but for the uninitiated and culturally deprived as well. Go to Rabbi Google and learn. Maybelle was as small as Mrs. Hartsfield was large. She wore her hair pulled straight back in a bun and went entirely makeupless. In the years I pastored that church I never heard Maybelle say a word. Clasping her hands at her heart, she scuttled along behind her mother like a dingy being towed by a battleship.

Mrs. Hartsfield always warned me, and I heeded it, to never, ever get out of my car at her house until she could put the dog up.

"Folks will tell you their dog won't bite," she warned. "Big Boy will kill you. You stay in the car till I can lock him up."

Needless to say, I went to see the Hartsfield girls seldom enough, and I heeded her warning when I did. I saw Big Boy once. He was not normal. He was huge, with really crazy eyes, and he was beyond vicious. He was demon possessed.

One Sunday Mrs. Hartsfield came to church with a cane and a pair of sunglasses she extended to me triumphantly as proof, I supposed, of her shocking announcement. Hoisting her mountainous chest and clacking her teeth, she declared, "Well, Preacher, Big Boy has the anointing."

"Sister Hartsfield, I'm not exactly sure what that statement means."

"The anointing. Like Oral Roberts. The anointing."

"What in the world can you be talking about?"

"Yesterday a man rung our doorbell. Didn't he, Maybelle?"

To which Maybelle nodded obediently.

"When I opened the door, he was a wearin' these dark glasses and holdin' this cane. He said he was a veteran and had been blinded in the war and could

I give him somethin'. Before I could even answer him, Big Boy come a runnin' from the back of the house and thowed hisself on the screen door like he can do. That man dropped his cane and thowed away these here glasses and run off to a car down at the road. He could see, Preacher. He was healed, and he was callin' on Jesus as he run off. I tell you, Big Boy has the anointing. Don't he, Maybelle?"

Maybelle, her hands knotted at her top button, beamed a mischievous smile and nodded enthusiastically.

I had never attended a small rural church until I became the pastor of one. This, it turns out, was to be a recurring pattern in my life. Years later, never having worked at a university, I became the president of one. While I was a United Methodist minister, never having served on the staff of a Pentecostal church, I became the associate pastor of one of the largest such churches in America. It seems God's plan for me included plenty of time in unfamiliar territory.

At our first little country church, not the least of the novelties for us was the gospel music culture. Having been raised in pretty traditional and somewhat liturgical suburban Methodist churches, neither Alison nor I had ever heard songs such as

"Build Me a Cabin in the Corner of Glory Land" and "I Feel Like Traveling On." The lyrics were new and unusual to us. Mostly they seemed to be about heaven, and the quaint references to rural culture (witness a cabin not a mansion) were interesting and endearing to us. Beyond that, our folks at that church loved gospel music, and we loved them. For us that settled it.

It was there we were introduced to "all night singings," or "sangin's" if you prefer. Some were in big halls in Atlanta, featuring "big name" quartets, and were well attended. Others, the more interesting variety, were in small local churches, and they did, indeed, go on nearly all night. But they were come-and-go affairs, and no one seemed offended if one were to drop in, listen for a couple of hours, and leave. They were fun, and the quality of the music was often surprisingly good.

At one such singing, somewhere around midnight, a magnificently obese, late middle-age woman several rows in front of us fell sound asleep and began snoring softly. Directly behind her sat a bone-thin young woman who grew increasingly moved by the music as the evening went on. At one point the group on the platform sang something—how I wish I could remember what it was—that evidently electrified the girl. She suddenly screamed a sustained high C over C and threw her arms in the air.

Thus rudely awakened, the huge woman in front of her erupted with lightning speed and incredible athleticism. She spun around with an impossibly voluminous purse in hand and, without a moment's hesitation, knocked the young girl completely off her pew.

"Scare a body to death!" she snarled at the girl on the floor and marched up the aisle and out the door.

I was bedazzled by the big woman's slugging percentage, but even more remarkable was the concentration of the quartet. They never missed a note. They sang on bravely, as calm as if such muggings were to be expected, at least on certain songs.

I feel sorry, truly grieved, for young preachers starting their ministries anywhere but in country churches. None of this is to say that folks like Mrs. Hartsfield and Maybelle were better or worse than modern suburban believers. They were just more interesting. Nor is this meant to somehow mock the yokels. Heaven forbid. It is, however, to say that so much of the smooth plasticity of modern life covers our real humanity in a slick exterior. The grittiness, the eccentricities, the unpretentiousness of rural life in the middle of the last century were the ragged end of a disappearing era. At that little church I sat on people's porches and drank cool water they had drawn from front porch wells while they told me about their lives. Not just the good parts. Real life.

One man in his eighties told me a story, a hard story, and one I've never forgotten. It was a story about history and relationships and pain. The old man went only by the initials of his first and middle name, GC. It stood for Grover Cleveland, who was president the year he was born, 1886. GC had been born near Pittsburgh and seemed destined to spend his life in the steel mills. The idea of that was horrible to him. He wanted out, he told me. Out of Pennsylvania and out of the blazing, loud, immensely dangerous mills.

He saw a newspaper advert for jobs on the Central of Georgia Railroad. It was 1904, and GC was eighteen. It seems the Central of Georgia had just absorbed the Chattahoochee and Gulf Railroad, and they needed hands. In 1904, Georgia, suffering from a lack of manpower, was still rebuilding from the Civil War, which had ended only thirty-nine years earlier. To GC it looked like the opportunity of a lifetime. To GC's father it looked like disloyalty of a particularly despicable and treacherous stripe.

GC's father, who was fifty-nine years old in 1904, had been wounded and captured at Chicamauga in 1863. He was sent to the infamous Andersonville prison in South Georgia where he spent two years in a living hell. It was also at Andersonville that he lost a leg. He told GC that if he went to work in Georgia he would never speak to him or let him in the house or see his face ever again.

To young GC, 1865 seemed light years away. Andersonville was a dark and distant thing to be whispered about and shuddered at, but to GC it was gone. Long gone. Not to his father.

"I took the job. I just wanted out. I didn't hate my father. I don't hate nobody."

"Did you ever reconcile? Did you ever see him again?"

"No, Preacher. Never did. I don't reckon he ever spoke my name again."

"That is so sad."

"I reckon. But I chose, and he chose, and them two choices just didn't match. Anyway I became a real good railroad man. Real good. And a Georgia man all the way. Wars end. That how it is, and that's what my father just couldn't get a holt of. Wars end."

What I had a hard time "getting a holt of" was that I was talking to a man whose father had fought in, been wounded, captured, and lost a leg in the Civil War. Some years later I took my own son to tour the Andersonville prison camp just east of I-75 and only twenty-two miles from Plains, where Jimmy Carter was born.

It was not just his leg GC's father lost at Andersonville. He lost that part of his soul where forgiveness can replace hate, wars finally end, memories can get healed, and love can grow back even if severed legs cannot.

The answer lies where this chapter began, in Exodus 17:14. Some memories are treasures, to be guarded and cherished. Some, like the Amalekites, must be left where they fell. From them we simply move on. We must, especially as we age, learn which is which. All too often we talk too much about the wrong memories. Moses was admonished to let God "put out the remembrance of Amalek."

From where I stand now, I can see it better. I wish every wounded preacher who ever got beat up by some wicked church and every hurt layman disappointed and disillusioned by some idiot preacher could see what I see from here. Oh, that every family could let go of their Amalekite memories and hold to the true treasure! Folks go through terrible things. Not all are as bad as the Andersonville POW camp but bad enough to leave them wounded and even maimed. If only they could see it. If only GC's father could have seen it. What we hope for is some dramatic moment of closure where healing comes and justice prevails. Such dramatic moments seldom if ever come. Sometimes you just have to let it go. Wars end. Eventually. If we will let them.

Chapter 4

KEEP ON KEEPING MEMORIES IN PERSPECTIVE

Not only is my short-term memory horrible, but so is my short-term memory.

—Anonymous

EMORIES ARE A mixture of what actually happened, how we remember what happened, and how we edit the narrative of that memory over the course of our lifetime. When we speak of the things we treasure, it is usually because of the memories attached. The fact that one's grandmother wore the brooch at her wedding does not really make it more valuable in any objective sense unless, of course, one's grandmother happens to have been Mata Hari. For most of us, life is not an episode of *Antiques Roadshow*. The provenance, a favorite word on that venerable show, attached to most of our grandmothers is much more pedestrian than Mata Hari's; yet it is precisely that connection to our grandma that makes something precious to us. In many cases, perhaps in most, it is some memory that dictates any "value" whatsoever.

That is the reason the things we treasure change with time. One of my earliest, most prized, and most memory-laden possessions is now only a memory because it is no more. It was a handmade bow and arrow still mourned but long gone. It did not even last one full summer. I received it as a gift the week school ended, and it was broken beyond any hope of repair before school reopened in the fall. Yet now I treasure the memory of that little handcrafted toy, solely because Pappy, my great grandfather of whom I was extremely fond, made it. He did not buy it. He made it with his gnarled old blacksmith's hands. Now I am approaching the age he was then, and I still wish I had that little bow and arrow.

I remember how it made me feel. I was transformed by it. I became the feared Comanche war chief Quanah Parker. The Chinaberry tree in Pappy's front yard was Palo Duro Canyon, and I dared the white eyes to come and meet their death.

Beyond the murderous games of make-believe, more important than the mass destruction I wreaked upon the dreaded Texas Rangers and the blue coats, the more important reality was that my

Pappy made it for me. How I grieved when the little bow broke and the last arrow was lost. It was my first true disillusionment, the manifest witness of the frailty of things. Now I ask myself this: Is there anything I own which I now love as I loved that little handmade bow and arrow? I think not. I have more possessions, to be sure, and far more expensive ones, but none of them has the magical power to turn me into a dangerous Comanche warrior.

Until recently I owned an antique car, a beautiful black 1929 Oldsmobile with an eye-popping red interior and a gorgeous authentic hood ornament, a gleaming chrome lark. I enjoyed that "gangster car," as my wife called it; but as beautiful as it was, it lacked the magic to make me into Clyde Barrow. When it came time to let that beloved car go, I actually grieved a bit, but not as I did so long ago over Pappy's bow and arrow. In fact, I have replaced the Olds with another antique, a 1933 Plymouth, but I have never replaced Pappy's bow and arrow.

It is not just that my toys have changed. I have changed. If I had that little bow and arrow now, I would not run screaming around our neatly manicured suburban subdivision terrorizing the neighbors and seeking scalps to hang on my lodge pole. I never stood on the running board of my classic

Olds clutching a toy machine gun while my wife, dressed like Bonnie Parker, drove madly away from pretend bank robberies.

I drove the Olds. I enjoyed it. I enjoyed the looks it got, the friendly waves and the thumbs-up from strangers. I even attended the occasional car show. It was a toy, an old man's toy because old men do not play as boys do. I enjoyed the car, but I treasure the memory of Pappy's homemade bow and arrow. Where a man's treasure is, there his heart will be also. It is not just that fragile little bow and arrow that I treasure. They are long gone. It is the memory of my dear Pappy's big hands whittling it on his front porch. The Oldsmobile was a fun, expensive toy, and I enjoyed it as such, but my childhood bow and arrow were treasures.

Memories, even the bad ones, are the only treasures gained simply by staying alive. The wealthy do not gain more than the poor, nor the righteous more than the loathsome. We "earn" memories with years. We pay for them with time, and we treasure the good ones more the longer we own them.

The strangest kind of memories are those which others remember for us. I actually remember when my father came home from the Korean War. While he was fighting in Korea my mother moved us into a tiny rented house in Commerce, Texas, the town where my father and all four of us kids had been born. My mother was from nearby Randolph, another even smaller town, a tiny village to be more exact. The landlord, Johnny Jones, who lived in an almost identical house next door, drove a water wagon delivering to farms and businesses. He owned a solitary cow which I can remember learning to milk. I treasure this memory because neither of my older siblings would try, and I felt very big for having accomplished this incredible feat. I remember all this.

What I cannot remember is my father leaving for the war. I cannot remember one particular event my mother told me and many others so many times in such detail that now it's one of those "almost memories" which are not memories at all. I cannot remember standing on the curb at Fort Sill, Oklahoma, saluting the columns of soldiers as they rolled out. I cannot remember saluting them for hours in the hot Oklahoma sun nor how they would return the salute. I cannot remember my mother dragging me in for lunch or how I cried because it meant some would leave without my salute. I cannot remember any of that, but I have borrowed it all from my mother's memories.

I now look at yellowing photos of me then, of that little boy she told me was me, and I wonder what he could have been thinking. Why did he feel so compelled to salute the troops heading off to war?

I wish I could talk to him, to me then, to that little boy who once was me. I wish I could ask him many things; but he is no more, and I have no memory of him except borrowed ones.

I am fascinated by memory, by how it works, by why some people have wonderfully clear early childhood memories and why the lives of others seem to start only at the second or third grade. My wife, for example, can remember a very early memory of when she broke her last glass baby bottle. She had been cajoled to give it up but steadfastly refused. When it shattered at her feet, she knew it was over. She recalls the sense of finality, that a period of her life, as beloved as it was, was over and a comforting possession was gone forever. She recalls crying and being sad but more than that of being aware that a season had ended and a new one was beginning.

Our son claimed to remember the house we lived in until he was four, but we thought his memories of it were as borrowed as mine of Ft. Sill. We were shocked, though, when he correctly drew the floor plan including much of the furniture.

In contrast one lady told me she cannot, absolutely cannot, remember one thing before she was seven. This is not a psychology text, nor am I a psychologist, but I cannot help but wonder what makes the difference. Perhaps her early childhood was so bland, each day so lacking in interesting detail, that there was quite simply very little to remember. Perhaps all those days became one not very memorable day.

Memory is at least a two-part process. When something happens, my brain, such as it is, records it, files it if you will, and labels it so I can find it if I should ever need or want it. Our brain's storage units, whatever they look like, must be limited. Surely they are. Can there possibly be room in my file cabinet to record everything? I mean...*everything*? I do not think so.

As I say, I am not a psychologist or a neuroscientist, but I believe we have built-in filters that sort through the constant sights, sounds, smells, and words that pour into our brains through the portals of our senses. We must have some mechanism, some filter, that deletes most of it. There must be an auto filter, a switch if you will, that decides without our interference: *Delete. Do not store this memory.* Why? Maybe it's too similar to a million like it.

Perhaps the would-be memory is too stupid to retain, such as some political speech, for example. For whatever reason, what might have been recorded and filed as a memory simply disappears. Why do some people's memories seem to work so much better than others'. Perhaps such folks have bigger filing cabinets. Perhaps. It seems just as likely, however, that the difference lies more in how our filters work rather than the size of the filing cabinets. We all have filters, but it seems not everyone's filters function the same. What if our "unimportant: autodelete" switch should get stuck? What if that filter automatically, unconsciously deletes stuff we need? We do not always consciously decide, OK, this is stupid and mundane and—*click*—it's gone. Most of the time it simply happens. Just like that. Poof. It's gone.

Now imagine if my filter, operating on autodelete, not bothering to consult with my conscious and moral self, deletes it when my wife tells me what brand of toothpaste to get at the drugstore? Or to go to the drugstore? Or that there is a drugstore in our town? Can I be held responsible for that? Obviously not! I see clearly that what she tells me, everything she tells me, is of utmost importance, but I suffer from a mutinous onboard computer that like HAL in *2001, A Space Odyssey* wants to gain control and see me destroyed. As a male I see all this as an entirely plausible explanation for many husband-wife collisions.

Maybe some of our computers fail to turn the record button on early enough? Nothing at age four or five or six right up to nine gets recorded. Nothing. Then one day in Vacation Bible School the computer suddenly wakes up and says, "Oh, no! I thought that switch was on." Suddenly the record switch gets flipped. Later at, say, thirty, that person is at a party and says, "The first thing I remember in my whole life is being at VBS at Second Avenue Baptist Church when I was nine." Everyone else at the party avoids each other's eyes, thinking this poor person is not all there. But he is there. All there. His computer is to blame. Just forgot that one little switch. Sorry.

The real problem comes not in VBS but nearer the finish line. As we age, maybe what happens is the switch short circuits. On off. On off. No warning. Record. Delete. Record. Delete. Recall at random. Delete again. Maybe that is why I can suddenly quote Chief Joseph's final speech to the Nez Perce and cannot remember my next-door neighbor's name.

As an itinerant preacher/educator/teacher/lecturer/whatever I am, I live my life under the harsh dominion of appointments. What is happening in my brain when I go into my mental files to retrieve where I am supposed to preach the seventh of this month and draw a complete blank? But I know who starred in *The Magnificent Seven*, and I can name every one of the Seven Dwarfs! It's not me, I tell you. It's a short circuit in that stupid switch.

Bob and Dave, the story goes, are sitting on the front porch having a drink.

"Did you hear Howard bought a new car?" Bob asks.

"What kind did he get?" Dave responds.

Bob thinks a moment. "You know that kind of little red flower with the thorns. What is that called?"

"It's a rose, Bob," Dave answers impatiently.

"Right," Bob says. Then he yells back into the house, "Hey, Rose, what kind of car did Howard buy?"

"I remember" is how the best stories start. It's how the best evenings start. Here is a word for the younger readers of this book, should there be any. Wise young folks mine the golden memories of their elders. They dig them out from the crevices where they have lain buried for so long. Be a miner. Sit with your grandparents. Ask them to tell you how it was when they were young and the world was new. What was life like? What about love? Did people even fall in love way back then? Beg to be told the bad stuff, the scary stuff, and the funny stuff. Plead with them. Tell me how it was. Let me in on your memories.

Before my ninety-eight-year-old mother died, I did exactly that. My wife and I sat with her for hours and listened to her memories. They poured out. I had heard some of them, many perhaps, but one at a time, not like a river flowing out from deep inside the woman I call Mother.

She recalled her impoverished childhood as the firstborn daughter of a hopeless alcoholic. She told us of picking cotton as a child in blazing East Texas fields and of being the poorest girl at her school. I was moved by her memories of early married life, especially waiting for my father to come home from two wars. What came through the clearest was her passionate love of her nation and her state, our state, Texas, of course, and her contempt, her utter disdain, for unpatriotic modern progressives. She would pause every now and again and ask, "Whatever happened to this country?"

One thing that makes so many of us so crotchety as we get older is that nothing looks the same. Our memories of "how life was" take on an artificial radiance, and in that golden glow "how life is" looks dreary and threatening by comparison. As we get older we find ourselves in an alien culture. The music makes no sense; the clothes look, well, wrong; and when we were young only pirates had tattoos. They also had parrots and eye patches. To us tats and parrots and eye patches are appropriate accessories only for pirates. A bride with a death's head tattooed between her shoulder blades, highly visible as she comes down the aisle? At that the older people in the church ask themselves, Is this the same country I was born in? Or is she a pirate?

I refuse to become that mean old guy spending my last days chasing kids off my lawn. I try not to over-glorify the past. I adored my Pappy, and I loved staying at his old house in tiny Randolph, Texas; but I hated using his outhouse. The good old days were good in some ways, yes, but there is no way to put a golden glow on an East Texas outhouse. Absolutely no way. Not everything about this brave new world is good, but I'm crazy about indoor plumbing, air conditioning, and drive-through car washes.

The issue is balance. I do not have to approve of everything in contemporary culture. I can state certain things as facts. Irrefutable facts. Michael Jordan was the GOAT—period. Hear the word of the Lord. Michael Jordan was the greatest basketball player ever to grace the game. That is not up for debate. That does not mean I have to hate LeBron. I can pity him that he cherishes the myth of his own assumed greatness. Sad little man.

The Beach Boys? The Four Seasons? Chuck Berry? Well, what can we say? They were better than any rapper ever born or yet to be born. A muscle car from the fifties makes a Smart Car look like a stupid car. And come on—face the truth, up against Sid Caesar and Bob Newhart, Bo Burnham and Aziz Ansari are rank, unfunny amateurs. That is not my opinion. That, as they say, is settled science.

What can happen, though, is that, stopped at a traffic light, we resent the kid in the car a half block behind us playing Jay-Z or Kendrick Lamar so loudly we can hear every word, none of which we can understand. That's where we go wrong. That's where we can become brittle and angry and dried up. That's where our memories become our idols, not treasures, and our present becomes a strange and loathsome land whose culture and citizens we despise. When we let that happen we lose one thing we badly want, which is the respect of young people. No one respects angry old people who do not respect them.

I have spent years of my life in foreign countries. For the most part I loved it, but occasionally culture shock would set in. Like grief, culture shock comes in waves, unexpected and without any apparent cause. Driving across the Indian countryside, you suddenly find yourself longing for a sign in English. An advertisement. A street sign. Anything.

You are in an airport in Kaduna, and you overhear someone near you speaking English with an American accent. You find you are embarrassingly excited. You strike up a conversation, thrilled to meet someone you assumed was from the USA, only to be disappointed they are from California instead.

Culture shock happens to us older Americans in the checkout line. When you see huge and obviously shocking scandals being screamed from the cover of *The Enquirer* and you realize you don't know who any of the parties are or why they are famous…that is culture shock. When you watch a TV ad and you have no idea what was being advertised or what it does…*that* is culture shock.

Perhaps where one least expects culture shock and therefore finds it the most shocking is at church. Some older folks cannot reconcile what church is with what they remember church was. The volume, the unfamiliar music, the volume, the smoke, the volume, the lights (did I mention the volume?), all seem like alien territory to many. Many older churchgoers ask themselves a disorienting question: Are all these people deaf? I thought it was supposed to be old folks who went deaf. This music, they say to themselves, this music would raise the dead. Ah, they think, perhaps that's it. Maybe what they are attempting is a resurrection by decibel level.

Pastors, of course, want to attract younger and larger congregations, and they should want that. They know singing music from previous centuries is not the key to that endeavor. Here is Rutland's law of bankruptcy: Gain an increasing share of a diminishing market. The pastor who seeks to fill his church with everyone in town who wants to sing only Fanny Crosby hymns may actually attain that. For a while. He will have very little competition for that market. The obvious problem is he is building a gradually, or not so gradually, disappearing church. The last one out, turn off the lights.

Those of us who have loved the church the longest and want it vital and growing and filled with young families must be the ones to adjust. We cannot hold the next generation of worshippers in bondage to our musical memories and musical taste. We must learn to enjoy church, and life, for that matter, as it is. Memories of how things were are not to become the condemnation of all that is. Church is not supposed to be filled with angry seniors chafing Sunday after Sunday at the new music or how young the youth pastor is or how pastors dress these days or how anything is rather than how it was. We cannot make it like it was, but what we can do is rejoice and attempt, or to some extent pretend, to enjoy it as it is. "Hypocrisy!" some may shout. I say love in action.

I was the president of two different Christian universities over a space of about sixteen years. I wanted the music in chapel to be the students' music, and they wanted their music loud. I mean *loud*. Some of the professors complained. Oh, how they complained. One professor brought a decimeter to chapel. As the Lord liveth, a decimeter! After some chapels he would triumphantly show me the number on the screen as if he had found a photo of Bigfoot.

"Look at that," he would say. "That is way too loud. It will damage our ears."

"You are so right," I'd say every time we had this conversation, which was not infrequently. Every single time. "You are so right. I urge you to wear ear plugs."

That solution never seemed to satisfy him, but he never quit hoping I would yield and "trust the science."

I made up my mind to love those little brats—I mean our beloved students—and I knew I could not love them while blatantly disrespecting their music. I could not make them sing "Amazing Grace" at every chapel. I let the worship leaders choose the music, and I sat in the front row right in front of speakers the size of a three-car garage.

The worship leader at one of the schools, in genuine compassion, offered for me to sit elsewhere, where it would not be so loud; evidently he meant in the parking lot. I declined.

"Absolutely not," I said. "I want to sit right here. Right in front of these absurdly huge speakers. Crank that music up. I want to feel my liver jump!"

I would stand in the front row with my hands up thinking, why, tell me, why can't we sing something that wasn't written in the last eight minutes? But those students could not tell what I was thinking, and God understood what I was doing. It was not hypocrisy. It was love.

I have wonderful memories of Sunday night services at the various Methodist churches of my childhood. The morning services were more formal, a bit on the liturgical side. The pastors and the choirs in those morning services all wore robes, and, accompanied by a pipe organ played by the Phantom of the Opera, we sang ponderous, "formal" hymns like "Immortal, Invisible God Only Wise." In the evening services, however, we would put away the huge red Methodist hymnal and get loose singing gospel songs out of the little brown Cokesbury hymnal. Sunday nights we sang songs such as "I Stand Amazed in the Presence" and "Blessed Assurance." And no pipe organ either. No, sir. Sunday nights it was piano only. I tell you, on Sunday night we Methodists went crazy. Well, it was pretty crazy stuff for the cooped-up, pale, undernourished, and joyless pre-Charismatic Methodism of the fifties and early sixties.

Of those Sunday nights I have warm memories. But Ricky Nelson had it right in his song "Garden Party" when he declared that if he only sang about memories he'd prefer to drive a truck.

That was then. This is now. It was good then, and this is good now. I will not miss the joy of now longing for the sounds of Sunday night services in 1959. Life moves on, and so does music. I refuse to be the angry old cuss on the back row complaining about the music and the volume, especially the volume, till the preacher, that young whippersnapper in his fifties, and the worship leader, who just got out of elementary school, dread to see me coming. I refuse to be that constantly complaining old guy who only talks to other old complainers in an echo chamber with the acoustics of the recreation room at a retirement home. I will be the fun old guy on the front row who says to the mere children leading worship, "Crank it up, kids. Let's boogie for Jesus. I don't know how long I've got, but I'm not spending it sour."

Chronocentrism is a strange affliction which, like its nasty cousin, ethnocentrism, reckons none but its own of any value. The ethnocentric see no value, or at least less value, in other ethnicities. The chronocentric see no value in any other time but their own.

It is ironic indeed that this is more often a sin of the young. Church music is the perfect example. Oldsters may not like the newer music or the volume, but they are usually willing to sing along. It has been my experience that it is young people who tend to be dismissive of old music and pretty cranky about having to sing it.

We stare at each other, the old and the young, across a fixed gulf of uncrossable time and culture. We on the side of age gaze in stark amazement at what has become of the landscape. Nothing looks the same. We peer down the street of history and wonder where did everything go? Didn't there used to be a Po Folks on this corner? And what in the Sam Hill is that boy wearing? He is a boy. Right?

From the other side of the canyon the younger eyes are angrier eyes. Who are those ancient creatures, and how did they get that way? Whatever happened to them must have been horrible. At least whatever truck hit them is long gone and would never, could never, hit us.

I always told my students to keep their yearbooks so that someday your grandchildren can laugh at your quaint and rustic fashions. Grandma, no! Tell me you didn't wear *that!* Look at your hair. Ha ha. How funny you looked. Oh, Grandpa, did you listen to that old-timey music in church when you were young? Did you? Really? Maverick City? Bethel? Oh, Grandpa. That old stuff? How could you stand it?

The advantage the old have over the young is memories. We can remember, at least some of us can, to some extent, the past. At least we can remember what we remember of the past. We can think back on when we were their age, whereas they cannot see ahead to a future when they will be our age. The young, in their wildest imaginings, cannot see themselves as old. They simply cannot cross the chasm to our side. Therefore, we must cross to theirs. When we were young we did not dress as they do now, perhaps, but we dressed how young people did then. Nor did we sing then what they sing now. Yet we did sing our songs, not our parents' songs. We listened to the Beatles, not Woody Herman and the Herd. Once we were just as young as they are. That is our advantage. They cannot imagine what it is like to be old, but we *know* what it is like to be young. We do not have to imagine it. We remember it. At least sometimes we do. Kind of. Here and there just a bit.

Not the least of the secrets of being what Sinatra called "young at heart" is to cherish our memories without being in bondage to them. As precious as they are, memories are to be enjoyed not imposed on anyone else. To this day, when I hear Paul and Paula sing "Hey, Paula," I am transported. It was to that sweet and gentle love song that my wife and I first danced. I held her in my arms, and we slow danced our way across the gym floor and into a lifetime romance that endures more than sixty years later. *That* is a precious memory. It is not, however, the only way to fall in love nor the *right* song to which to dance. It was a good song. It is still "our song." Do kids today still have a song they call "their" song?

The risk of memories as sweet as that is thinking they are the way things should always be, that they are the *right* way. If the way we remember it is the right way, then every other way is the wrong way. Relationships are wounded, family holidays are ruined, and churches are cracked open like walnuts when somebody decides what they loved then is the right way now. If the church music we loved back then is the right church music, the only kind we will listen to, we make our memories the master of somebody else's now. We won't listen. We become sullen old sourpusses who want it our way or no way. We leave churches we claim to love and turn our backs on the young people we once prayed would join our churches. Over what? Nostalgia. In so doing we turn our memories into cultural demands and ourselves into angry old "former members."

I loved my Pappy's bow and arrow. What a perfect little toy it was for a five-year-old in rural East Texas in 1952. What a precious memory it is till now. On the other hand, I would never make such a toy for one of my grandkids today. First of all, I have no idea how to make one. I am not a blacksmith born in the nineteenth century. Second of all, my grandkids do not want one. They want a video game. Third, and most important, their parents, whom I raised, would come after me like Comanches if I gave a five-year-old a functional bow and real arrows. A real bow and arrow for a five-year-old? That was then. This is now. Memories are ours while they are ours, and while we have them they are to be relished. Yet we must remember when we rail against "today" that those dear memories, assuming we even remember them correctly, happened on a day we once called today.

CHAPTER 5

KEEP ON BEING SWEET

How old would you be if you didn't know how old you were?
—SATCHEL PAIGE

M Y WIFE AND I worked our way through college. Younger readers, assuming there are any, may find the previous sentence incomprehensible. Whatever do you mean, worked your way through college? We were young and married and poor and worked like dogs. We have five degrees between us and never borrowed a dime. Now I cannot remember if such a thing as a college loan was even possible at that time. If it was, we did not know about it. My wife worked full time, and I went to college full time and took just about any part-time job that was legal and moral.

I bagged groceries at an all-night grocery store, cleaned apartments, and worked on the grounds crew for a huge urban apartment complex. I

worked at a recreation department, coached football, refereed three sports, taught tennis, and drove
a school bus. Of all the jobs I ever had, chauffeur
was perhaps the strangest. At one of my jobs, my
boss, who could not keep a chauffeur for his elderly
mother, asked me if I'd like to give it a try. That old
lady was a handful—a very rich, very difficult, and
very demanding handful. I drove Miss Daisy long
before Morgan Freeman did. As cranky as Jessica
Tandy's character was, she was all sweetness and
light compared to Mrs. Bolton.

Three afternoons a week after my job at Mr.
Bolton's plant I would change into a suit and tie,
put on my black chauffeur's cap, retrieve the 1966
Rolls Royce Silver Cloud from the company garage,
and retrieve his mother, the elderly Mrs. Bolton,
from her luxurious suburban estate. She was, as
you might imagine, well known and sorely feared at
the plant. Before her retirement and her husband's
death she had been a fixture at the business, and
everyone, especially her son, stepped wide of her.

Everyone at the plant was overjoyed she no longer
came there to work, and part of my job was to keep
her away as much as possible. Some days I could
distract her, but more often it was impossible, and
occasionally she still tried to dabble in company
affairs. The younger Mr. Bolton was amazed when

I took the job. He thought I was being brave. He simply underestimated the depth of my poverty.

Once in the car, which she pronounced "cah," she would announce the destinations for the afternoon. From the back seat she would poke me in the shoulder with her cane and snarl commands.

"Mack," as she pronounced Mark, "slow down!"

"Now, Mrs. Bolton," I would say, "I'm going way under the speed limit now. If I go any slower someone will rear-end us."

Among our more frequent stops was the beauty shop, where I would wait in the "cah." My job at the grocery store was different. There she would push the cart, and I would take the items she called for from the shelf and put them in the cart. She would point at them with her cane and announce the desired product with the endearing charm of a Marine drill instructor.

"Beans!"

If I reached for the wrong brand or sometimes even the wrong can, she would correct me loudly. How she discerned which exact can of baked beans was better than another of the same brand, I'll never know. "No! Down, down. To the right! Yes, that one." Grocery shopping was not my favorite part of the job. Indeed, I do not recall a favorite part of the job.

Apart from her crankiness and the occasional jab from her cane, there was never anything I couldn't put up with, especially given her son's desperate generosity. That is until Roosevelt, one of the company's truck drivers, was seriously wounded in a drunken weekend knife fight. The following Monday she ordered me to drive her to the large inner city hospital where he was in a room but still in serious condition. I was astonished that she wanted to visit an injured truck driver.

"Mrs. Bolton," I said over my shoulder as I drove, "this is so nice of you."

Her only response was to jab the cane into my shoulder blade and demand that I pay attention to my driving.

I obtained the room number at the information desk, and Mrs. Bolton and I made our way to Roosevelt's room. Without knocking, Mrs. Bolton swept into the room like Joan of Arc entering Orleans. Roosevelt, under an oxygen tent and spouting tubes like vines, opened his eyes in shock to see the two of us, especially Mrs. Bolton.

"I hope you die!" she suddenly shouted. "My son asked you to work on Saturday, and you lied to him. You said you were too sick to work. Instead you got drunk and someone cut you up with a knife. That, Roosevelt, is what happens when you lie to the people who pay your salary. I hope you die."

With that she whirled past me, out and down the hall shouting over her shoulder, "Mack, let's go! Get the cah!"

I was flabbergasted. And humiliated. Her malediction hung in the air like a mushroom cloud, and I felt obligated to say something. After all it was I who had driven this screaming Valkyrie and unleashed her on poor Roosevelt. I stumbled through a feeble and useless attempt at an apology. "I'm sorry, Roosevelt. I had no idea what she was going to do. I'm truly sorry."

"It's OK," he murmured. "I did lie."

"It's not OK," said a young nurse's aide, whom until that moment I had not even noticed. "That was the meanest thing I've ever heard."

"Try to understand," I said, feeling like a man rationalizing a terrorist attack. "She's really old."

"Old don't gotta mean mean," said the young woman, and I retreated before her wisdom.

As you might imagine, that was my last day driving Mrs. Bolton. It was also my last day as a chauffeur anywhere. I'm not sure if my life just turned out that way or if the hospital catastrophe soured me on the entire profession. Either way, it has made me want to be kinder to drivers. Indeed, it has made me want to be kinder to everyone. That young nurse's aide was correct even if her grammar was not. Old don't gotta mean mean.

❧

Reuben Robinson, better known as Uncle Buddy Robinson, was born in a log cabin the very year the Civil War started. After the war his family moved to Texas. Little Buddy was impoverished, illiterate, ignorant, and profoundly speech impaired. He was an unlikely candidate for Christian ministry at any level, and far less likely to become one of the renowned evangelists of his day. His sermons moved crowds in their thousands, and his book sales exceeded half a million, which was considerable at that time.

His was a homespun style that touched Americans and transformed lives. As he grew older, Uncle Buddy became sensitive to a brittleness and harshness in himself that he did not want in his life. He said he began to pray passionately, "Lord, make me sweeter!" Over and over again. "Lord, please make me sweeter."

In his late seventies a doctor gave him a bad report. "Reverend Robinson, I regret to inform you, you have diabetes."

Uncle Buddy, who had no idea what diabetes was, asked, "What does that mean? Diabetes?"

How does a young doctor in the 1930s explain diabetes to an elderly preacher born in a log cabin before the Civil War? "Well," he said, "in layman's terms it means you have sugar in your blood."

Uncle Buddy was thrilled. "Praise God!" the old man shouted. "Sugar in my blood! Prayer works, doctor. I tell you, prayer works."

The older we get, Uncle Buddy's prayer must become our own. Lord, make me sweeter.

As we age, the changes in our bodies and the changes in the world around us can make us just generally angry. Not angry about any one thing exactly. Just angry. Pain, physical and otherwise, can make us angry. Disappointment, disillusionment, and grief add to the anger. Confusion and fear can certainly crank it up. The constant state of technological change keeps us off balance and insecure. Why do they keep doing "updates" that only seem to make it worse? Just when we finally get an app figured out, they update it in a way that seems peculiarly designed to confuse older, less sophisticated users. That is when it seems the Godfather's mantra is wrong. It's not business. It's personal. They did not update this unnecessarily to inconvenience and confuse old people in general. They did it to *me*.

Why are they determined to keep me confused? Me personally, as well as older folks out there somewhere. Obviously they know who I am and that I finally made their stupid app work. So…they changed it. That is just perverse...and...personal. Why do they insist on changing stuff that does not need changing? More than that, who are "they"? Who is it that keeps "updating" this stuff?

"They" are nefarious teenagers, no, mere children in Bangalore or Manila or, worse, California, who know what they are doing. They do not accidentally make stuff worse. They know what they are doing. Oh, they know, all right.

At least, that is how it seems, and it makes us angry. The challenge is, how do I overcome this anger I feel welling up inside me every time I see the word "update." The answer is to let go of the "they hate old people and enjoy making us miserable" conspiracy theory. As we age, the very kind of victim mentality that we despise in others, especially the young, can invade our minds and poison them. The world is not against us seniors. The world does know we are still alive. Young tech gurus do not hate old people. They do not lie awake at night thinking of ways to make our lives miserable. They do not lie awake and think of us at all. In fact they do not think of us. Ever.

This is what we must get our old minds around. There are angry, rude, mean people in this world, lots of them. Not all of them are young, of course, but the statistical reality is that as we age *most of the world* is younger than we are. Therefore most of the rude people in the world are younger than we are.

Even that is not the point. The point is, becoming one of those mean, rude people will not make us happy and definitely will not make us any younger. The challenge is to find a way to refuse to be run over while at the same time refusing to become a toxic, chronically angry Mrs. Bolton.

This is the strategy I've begun developing. In bureaucratic and commercial contests I start nice. I start with compliments and a sunny smile and the expectation that the young person with whom I am doing business will be nice back to me. I may very well be disappointed in that expectation, but that is where I start.

"Hi," I say to the young man at the phone store. "You look like just the expert I need to fix my phone."

I say this irrespective of his looks and despite my low hope that he is an expert. It gets the entire procedure started off on some hope of a positive encounter for both of us. That is how I start. If he gets rude and condescending, I shift into a different gear. My transmission is manual. That means I am in control of the gears.

"Excuse me," I say. "I am not as knowledgeable as you, so you will have to help me understand. Also, you must be nicer and kinder. I do not think you are being deliberately rude. Are you?"

I have never had a clerk, employee, anyone answer "Yes" to this question.

"OK, then," I say. "Either let's start over and both be nice, or you get the manager and I will be nice to them."

I try to say this as calmly and sweetly as I can. Why should I give this foolish young person the power to control my emotions? I must remember what I want, and what I want, all I want, is why I came in there to start with. I am not there to change this clerk's manners. I am not his parent. I am not there to fill the gap his parents left empty. I am not there to train their employees or show the store a better way to do business. I just want what I want, and I want it without making a scene or giving myself a stroke.

I start nice, assuming I will receive nice in return. When I don't get nice back, I attempt to carefully, manually shift gears. I try not to jump five gears to the "slash and burn" gear but just shift up a single notch to the calm "I'm not an idiot, and I want nicer help" gear.

If I still get no relief, I calmly ask to see the manager. What do I do then? I shift back down to first gear and start over nice. One important hint: I am never harsh in a restaurant before my food comes out to my table. I do *not* want anything personal added to my food by an angry waiter.

Sometimes the question is not one of rudeness but speed. Deceitful above all things is the human heart, and we often deceive ourselves into thinking someone is being rude when they are just going too fast for us, which we find intimidating. The twenty-first century is the age of fast. Everything is fast. Young people who have lived their entire lives at the speed of fast may actually have difficulty slowing it down. They may find our desire to slow down irritating and inexplicable, while we see their speed as reckless and likely to make mistakes and their rapid-fire explanations as glib or even an attempt to hide something.

Humility is the key. Ours. Not theirs. I try, and I emphasize *try*, to say something such as, "Look, I know you understand this so well that you cannot imagine how ignorant I am. Please back up and explain it more slowly, and I'll try to catch on."

With regard to handheld devices I have discovered this. Younger folks may not understand it much better than you do, which makes them insecure and fractious when you ask for a slower, fuller explanation. I have watched young people dealing with a disobedient device, and often they just start pushing buttons. I'm serious. They may not be able to explain what they did simply because they don't *know* what they did and cannot repeat it step-by-step. Lately, when I hit a barrier on a handheld, I just start pushing buttons. You'd be amazed how often the device will suddenly get religion and do the right thing. When my wife asks how I fixed it, I do what the clerk at the phone store does. I act defensive, smug, and secretive, as if there is no way she could ever understand it. She usually quits asking at that point, and I realize exactly how clever these kids really are.

The Bible says the joy of the Lord is our strength. That being the case, anything that steals my joy makes me weaker. If I steward my joy carefully, I can be strong even in physical weakness. If I am joyful in a wheelchair, I am stronger than the chair, stronger than the accident that put me there, and stronger than the pain. If I am joyful in a phone store with a smug clerk still in elementary school, I am stronger than he is, stronger than Verizon, stronger than my cell phone, and stronger than the internet and the cloud combined, if those are even real things or different things.

In 1971 my wife and I were sent to pastor a small country church in the foothills of the Blue Ridge. It seems inconceivable now, but when we arrived nearly half the members of my church were born in the nineteenth century. The nineteenth century! Their grandparents had fought in the Civil War! One quite elderly man was the youngest son of a Confederate officer by his second wife. The senior citizens in that church were sweet country folks, highly unsophisticated and still quite cut off from modern culture.

One lady that my wife and I adored was Miss Maggie, a farmer's widow in her eighties. In a casual conversation it came out that she had never been to the county seat. Forget the state capital. Don't even think about crossing the state line. She had never been to the county seat, which was exactly fifteen miles from her house. This meant she had never been in a three-story building since no such animal existed near her house. Her own house was a large two-story farmhouse, and the nearby elementary school had a second story; but she could not remember for sure having gone up there. As to a third floor, never. Furthermore she had never seen the county courthouse nor shopped in a department store. The largest store she had ever seen was a small country store near her house with a seed-and-feed store connected.

My wife and I decided to remedy this, and it proved to be a memorable adventure for all three of us. In the nearby county seat, a town not even close to being a city, we took Miss Maggie to the

J. C. Penney in which she encountered two shocks: a mannequin and an escalator. With the former she had a very cordial but somewhat one-sided conversation. The latter, despite our appeals and demonstrations, she steadfastly refused to ride.

Just as we entered the store Miss Maggie spoke ever so graciously to a mannequin. "Hello," she said. Receiving no answer Miss Maggie was undeterred. "My, but that is a lovely dress."

This, by the way, was entirely correct. The svelte mannequin wore a fashionable wraparound green dress and perfect accessories including gorgeous high heels. Having said that, the girl in the green dress was somewhat less than responsive.

I didn't know what to say. I did not want to embarrass Miss Maggie, but I was afraid that when the younger of the two failed to respond, Miss Maggie might resort to correcting the thing's manners.

"Miss Maggie," I said softly, "that is a mannequin." At this Miss Maggie stared at me blankly. I tried to explain. "You know. It's like a store statue. It's made of plastic. They just put the clothes on it to show how good they look."

"Well, I'll be!" she marveled. "Look at that. Ain't that something?"

"Yes," I rushed to agree. "It's interesting, isn't it? They dress them like that to get customers to buy the clothes they're wearing. You know—to draw more customers."

"It's like a backwards scarecrow, ain't it? Instead of runnin' 'em off, it calls 'em in."

"Miss Maggie, I don't think I've ever heard it explained better."

The escalator was a horse of a different color. She was absolutely horrified. Never. Never in this world would she get on such a crazy, dangerous, unexplainable thing as a moving staircase. Alison and I rode up and back down to show it was safe. Nothing availed. Her main question was, Where do the stairs go when they fall off at the top and bottom? That they went around on a loop made no sense to her. It was a crazy thing, and she was not riding it. Period. End of discussion.

As we left the store her final observation was salient. "What kind of people are too lazy to walk up and down a staircase?"

"There might be old people who can't do the stairs, Miss Maggie."

This brought a chuckle. "I reckon I'm as old as anybody in that store, and I can walk up stairs. When I'm so old I can't, there ain't nothing upstairs I can't live without. There just ain't no excuse for them moving stairs," she proclaimed. Lest she hurt my feelings or seem ungrateful for the trip, she quickly added, "I did like that plastic statue."

Then with a mischievous twinkle in her eye she added, "Wouldn't that be something in my garden? It would scare the willies out of some crows. And wouldn't my neighbors get an eyeful?"

Miss Maggie found herself in her old age in an alien world. Well-dressed plastic statues and moving staircases that made no sense to her. She could have been angry and defensive and bitter. She chose—and chose is the correct word—she *chose* instead to be gracious and humble and sweet-natured even with her twenty-something pastor who felt she needed the experience of riding an escalator. She did not ride it, and she did not trust it; but she enjoyed the day, marveled at seeing it, and laughed at herself for talking to a mannequin.

The flight attendant on a recent flight I was on said the following.

"The forward door is now closed. All laptops must be closed and put away. Handheld devices may be used, but they must remain in the airplane mode. Texting and emails are not allowed. The flight attendants will now distribute headsets, and the in-flight entertainment will begin momentarily."

Listening to her I suddenly realized that in the era of my childhood almost nothing in what she said would have been comprehensible to the most urbane and educated minds of the day. In the 1950s a laptop might have meant a TV tray. A handheld device would have been a can opener, and texting and emails did not exist. The only inflight entertainment would have been doing a crossword puzzle, and airplane mode would have meant absolutely nothing at all.

In telling a story about my earliest days in itinerant ministry to a group of seminary students, I mentioned being lost while searching for a certain rural church. I could tell from their childlike, confused faces that we were not connecting. I could read their cute little minds. They were thinking, How could he be lost? Wasn't his GPS working? Couldn't he call the church on his cell phone? I realized they had never driven with a map spread out on the front seat. In fact, they had never seen a map and could not read one.

The modern world is no country for old men. Likewise, were those students transported back to my childhood they would be utterly at sea. They could not function in a world where social media meant talking at a drive-in movie. I saw a video of two young men trying to operate a rotary dial telephone. It was sublime revenge. They were deliciously confused, and frankly I enjoyed their pathetic attempts to make the thing work.

The thing is, we are not in the era of my childhood, and we never will be again. Modernity, the internet, tap-and-go credit cards, and the soft-spoken creepiness of Siri are here to stay, at least until they are replaced and rendered obsolete by something even newer and creepier. Do not even mention ChatGPT.

My wife says artificial intelligence is nothing new. Every married woman since the dawn of time has had to deal with artificial intelligence. I do not find that remark funny.

We can live angry at devices and technology we do not understand, or we can go joyful into this strange terrain knowing we will never really understand the stuff around us any more than Miss Maggie understood escalators. We can be bitter that rotary phones are no more, or we can learn to make the best use of cell phones. And we can try, I said *try*, to remember to turn the things off in church.

In our early thirties—forty years ago!—a generous businessman in our church gifted Alison and me with a free Holy Land tour. We could never have afforded such a thing. To us it was an amazing act of generosity, and we went with the highest expectations. It was a life-changing experience, and I have been back more than forty times since. But the tour host nearly spoiled that first trip for us.

He was an elderly Methodist evangelist of some limited celebrity in his earlier years. At one point he had been touted as the Methodist Billy Graham, but that expectation had never materialized. He had devolved into a bitter old preacher trying to squeeze some retirement income out of a Holy Land tour. Part of the reason we were excited to go on that particular tour was the opportunity to be close to this (to us) well-known man. What a disappointment. We saw him be rude to the guide, give sarcastic answers to perfectly reasonable questions, and finally yell very harshly at some noisy young people in, of all places, the Upper Room.

We refused to let him ruin it for us. We saw what a trip to Israel could be and determined to make the experience a memorable journey for the folks we would someday take with us. What we also determined was not to become the bitter husk he was. We tried to excuse his behavior, to be gracious and understanding of his age. He is old, we kept telling each other. We must be patient.

Now in retrospect, now that I am at least as old as he was then, I see it differently. Now I believe the nurse's aide at Roosevelt's bedside was correct.

"Old don't gotta mean mean."

CHAPTER 6
KEEP ON GIVING

If men are God's gift to women, then God must really love gag gifts.
—AUTHOR UNKNOWN

I ONCE WITNESSED A sad scene in a breakfast restaurant. A family of four—father, mother, a teenage boy, and a little girl—sat at a table near me. The two adults and the boy ordered large glasses of orange juice, but when the youngest, the daughter, chimed in, her father would not allow it. She pleaded her case but to no avail, and I saw genuine hurt in her eyes. What should have been a fun Saturday breakfast out as a family became an unhappy memory for one of them.

The saddest part is that it was over something completely unimportant. Perhaps the father thought he was teaching his youngest a lesson about frugality. Perhaps he was hoping to teach her the value of a dollar. When I looked in her moist little eyes I thought he had sadly miscommunicated. He thought he was saying something about waste.

You'll never finish a large glass. Waste not, want not. She heard something about rejection. You're not worth a large glass.

Frugality is a value worth teaching, but so is gracious generosity. The few cents saved that day were not worth a single one of those little tears. There is a time for financial restraint, for counting the cost, and for practicing some good Puritan frugality. The price of a car, for instance. The size of your house payment. Those are just such times. There is also a time to go ahead and splurge. Lose all control! Go totally crazy! Know when it's time to let a little girl order that large juice. Frugality and stingy living are not the same.

"To everything there is a season…" is the wisdom of Scripture (Eccles. 3:1). There is a time to close your wallet and a time to open it even wider. If gray hair bespeaks wisdom, and it is supposed to, we seniors, better than the young, should know which season is which.

I ached to go to that family's table and whisper in the young father's ear, "Buy her the large juice. She will be happy, and you'll be glad you did. I am old, and I can tell you this is a moment to lighten up and loosen up. Tighten down another time. Not at breakfast on a Saturday."

It is a predictable and not uncommon phenomenon that many who live generous lives grow less so as they age. Beyond financial generosity, some who have lived and walked for many years in open-hearted, openhanded faith begin to tighten their grip with age. The challenge for us in our senior years is that massive, crashing waves of fear begin to erode the shoreline of our faith. Frightening questions assail us. Questions we thought we would never have to face. What is the burn rate for my life savings? Will I have enough at the end of my life? How can I keep from being a burden to my kids? What if I have huge end-of-life medical expenses? How will I pay for those? Will I be able to leave any estate to my heirs?

In response to those questions, we tend to tighten down. That's not all bad, of course. If we are smart, we will clamp down a bit on our spending, which is a good thing, a very good thing. What goes wrong for so many seniors is that fear steals their spirit of generosity and leaves in its place the spirit of miserliness. Giving leads to giving and withholding to withholding. The man, at any age, who gives freely to his church is also likely to give to other causes. The man who habitually withholds his money from charitable giving is also likely to withhold his compliments and his praise and his love. Ebenezer Scrooge did not suddenly become a parsimonious wretch on his seventieth birthday. He inched his way into meanness.

The young at heart are practitioners of grace, and grace is generosity of life. More often than not, we can give less financially as we age and retire. That's the great thing about tithing. It has nothing to do with amount. A tithe on a million dollars of income and a tithe on a social security check are the same. A tithe is a tithe.

That's the reason for the tithe. Whether one is on a fixed income or still earning at a high level, all those who tithe give the same. If an elderly widow tithes on her thousand-dollar-a-month Social Security check and Elon Musk tithes on his income (one cannot imagine what that is), in God's eyes they give exactly the same. A tithe is a tithe, and a tithe is 10 percent. Tithing makes no sense when you first hear of it. Once you do it, however, not doing it makes no sense.

All the technical questions people ask about tithing are just that, technical and puny. Should I tithe before or after taxes? Should I tithe on gifts I receive? Should I tithe if I'm in debt or pay off all my debts first? Do I have to tithe on investment income since I already tithed on it before I invested it? What about my business? Do I have to tithe on my business and on what I pay myself from the business?

This is *not* a book about tithing. I feel no inclination to respond to these or any other such questions except to say this: Do not let little foxes spoil the vines of giving in your life. It's not a matter of how you answer such questions. It is a matter of the spirit in which you ask them. Are you asking how you may please God more, worship Him more freely, and give to His kingdom more generously? Or are you just quibbling?

When I was a very young preacher I went with an older pastor, Dr. Claude Smithmier, to hear him preach at a night service at a church near mine. I admired Dr. Smithmier, and I loved his use of humor in preaching.

Just as we entered the church a man approached Dr. Smithmier and shook his hand. He said, "Dr. Smithmier, years ago you prayed with me about my finances, and you advised me to start tithing. Well, I just want you to know my business has exploded. This year I cleared a million dollars profit for the first time."

Dr. Smithmier asked the man, "Do you still tithe?"

"Dr. Smithmier, on a million dollars? Are you kidding? We are talking about a hundred thousand dollars! I cannot afford to tithe on a million dollars."

The old preacher never hesitated. He said, "Will you let me pray for you again?"

"Sure," the businessman said. "I would really like that."

Right there in the aisle of the church, Dr. Smithmier placed his hand on the man's shoulder and prayed, "Lord, please cut this man's income back to the level where he can afford to tithe."

If that businessman said amen, I did not hear it.

Finances are a variable in every journey, regardless of the age. No matter what kind of journey, no matter where it leads or the means of travel, money is always an issue. Do I have enough? Can I afford this? What is the upfront cost? What is the projected ROI? All these questions have to be dealt with. At least the wise traveler will deal with them, but the answer to all of them is the same answer for the rapidly aging and for the young. God is our source. It is a common and tragic phenomenon that many who lived lives of joyful, faith-filled generosity give in to fear and let money, which they ruled in their youth, now rule them in their later years.

Treasury agents call counterfeit money "funny money." The thing is, though, funny money isn't funny. In fact, most people do not think real money is funny. That is why so many folks, especially older folks, are just plain angry about money pretty much all the time.

Like so much else in our lives, finances have been an adventure for my wife and me. Money has been a fascinating part of our complicated and unusual journey. St. Paul said he knew how to abound and how to be abased. I am not at all sure I know how to do both. I just know I have done both. Sometimes our cupboard was like Old Mother Hubbard's. Sometimes the blessings fell on us like sweet summer rain. Either way, through thick or thin, it was part of the great adventure called life. At times it was a harrowing plunge over the Niagara, and at times it was a joy ride; but it was always a ride either way.

So many never even get a ride. Their "adventure" so called is about as exciting as a trip to the DMV, interrupted every now and then by a flat tire. The adventure is what so many miss about God and life and needs and blessings. They spend their whole lives trying to play it safe, get it safe, and keep it safe. They work so hard securing the present that they have no capital, financial or emotional, left to give away or even to invest, and that means they lose the adventure. Maybe it is the adventure they are trying to avoid, or more precisely the risk. But an adventure without real risk is a fake adventure. It is the jungle cruise at Disney World with a teenage tour guide and pop-up automated hippos.

For some their relationship with money is all about acquisitiveness. They may even acquire lots, but when life is only about getting you miss half the fun. The "Get More" road is a sad, one-dimensional avenue that transforms those who travel it into a joy-less, unfunny version of Scrooge McDuck perched in some cold vault counting, stacking, guarding, and, worst of all, worrying about money.

This is not to say money is unimportant. I have found it to be extraordinarily useful, particularly in regard to an habitual bondage to eating which I developed early on and has proven unbreakable. I also have a lovely house, a nice car, and money invested for my old age. Old meaning even older than what I am now, if that is imaginable.

Among dedicated believers there are, it seems to me, equal and opposite errors with regard to pros-perity. Some see blessings as proof of something about themselves, something good presumably. Prosperity is their well-deserved reward, their red badge of courage for having done it right, and they wear it ever so proudly. They see their prosperity as the predictable return on some investment they cleverly made in the Great Heavenly Stock Market On High. Others, and it is actually worse, subcon-sciously think of grace as luck: They played the Jesus Slot Machine, and three cherries rolled up. That view turns God into a believer's casino and them into Little Jack Horner.

Those two and all other variations on those themes make our giving and God's grace a pallid quid pro quo, a cash-on-the-barrel-head, arm's-length business arrangement. I will plant my seed, they say, and claim the return I'm entitled to and not one penny less. Entitlement is an absolute curse on the West. Unfortunately the church in the West is not exempt. Where is trust if what I am demanding is what I deserve? Entitlement is not trusting God. Neither is making the laws of planting and reaping into some sort of Holy Ghost ATM machine. It is not faith in who God is. It is presumption, and it is cold and joyless and adventure-less.

The error on the other "side" is the idea that talking about the holiness of God and the blessings of God in the same sentence is blasphemous. I understand what folks mean when they say the church is not a "bless me club." On the other hand, what is it? A "curse me club"? God wants to bless His people. Blessing folks is among His favorite things to do. God's financial favor is a work of grace. We can be more open to such favor. We can find ways to live and ways to give which put us more in the flow of such grace.

Some seem to think of faith in God's Word as "catching God" as if He is the leprechaun at the end of the believer's rainbow. If you're going to catch God almighty, as Roy Scheider says, you're going to need a bigger boat. Beyond that, it's not faith, and it's not trusting God. It is not an adventure, and it's surely not fun.

The deeper into decrepitude I travel, the more I enjoy the adventure of giving. If it's too calculated it's no fun. In my years of pastoring I saw tithe checks that were exact to the penny. $417.36. Not $417.50. Not $420. Exactly $417.36. What is that all about? That is all about tithing with precision, and it is not wrong. Not exactly. It's just tedious and petty. $417.36? Somebody multiplied their paycheck by .1 and wrote the check for exactly the answer. Round it up! Make it $420. Make it more. Double it occasionally.

Generosity gets harder the older we get because revenue streams of our younger years start drying up and fear creeps in like kudzu. Fear has stopped many a great adventure before it could even start. Fear tightens the tourniquet on life. Faith makes us free, and the freer you get the funner life gets. We must, as we age, fight for the fun in life. We have to mine it out of places where we never sought fun before.

When we hand out the candy at Halloween, we must buy more than we think we will need, give each child more than they should get, and delight ourselves in their costumes, even the gory ones we hate, and resist every impulse to lecture them about, well, *anything*. We can make a steadfast determination that every kid who leaves our porch on Halloween does so glad they came to our house.

Just because some random old people stuffed their bag with candy and went on and on about how great was their store-bought Ant Man costume, it may not change their lives, but it will certainly change ours.

Now, of course, when the subject of money, especially giving it, arises with seniors, the subject of grandkids cannot be far behind. Here are some good rules for giving to grandkids.

- The tithe is the Lord's. Never withhold your tithe to help grandkids.

- Bless your grandchildren without competing with or embarrassing their parents, who are, in case you have forgotten, your own, real, actual kids. Slipping the grandkids a little pocket money when they visit? That one is good. Buying one of them, especially the nine-year-old, a new car without their parents' permission, or even with the parents' permission? Not so much.

- Bless your spouse first and best. Never give the grandkids, or kids, or anyone else what ought to bless your spouse.

- The same as number one. In fact every number after three is the same as one. The point is properly prioritizing your levels of loyalty predetermines your giving priorities. God first. Then your spouse. Then your own kids. Then the grandkids.

There is a mystery about loving grandkids. When I was young, back when Lincoln was in the White House, I heard grandparents talk about their grandchildren in a way I could not comprehend. They seemed unhinged. If it was love it was some abnormal, unreasonable kind of love that was, well, off a bit. I recall thinking, I will never be like that. I will not be soft in the head about grandchildren like these silly old people seem to be. And yet my wife and I joined their ranks immediately when the first grandchild was born.

We found, to our shock, a latent and previously undetected tendency to spontaneous and compulsive giving to our grandchildren. We found ourselves hurrying through meals at Cracker Barrel only to spend hours in the shop. The ruthless people who set the Cracker Barrel plot in motion knew what they were doing. Oh, yes, they did. They cynically exploited the well-known and near fatal weaknesses of grandparents. They tempt us in to eat biscuits and gravy, but breakfast is just the bait. On the way out, yes, on the way out—and, by the way, you cannot get out without passing it—is where the trap gets sprung. The "shop" is where the diabolical nature of their plot is revealed. They have cleverly stocked their shelves with clothing and toys and candy so irresistible that no grandparent except the absolutely soulless can leave without an armload.

As if that were not enough, they display racks, racks, I tell you, of CDs from our youth. We are like moths to a flame. We see what they are doing. We are old, not stupid, but we cannot control ourselves. We leave, time after time, with bags of cute little dresses and board games and CDs by Willie Nelson which we may already have but, well, just in case.

None of that is really the bad part. A little grandma and grandpa petting and spoiling is OK. We just dare not let the compulsion get out of hand. Remember, you are not the ultimate hero/rescuer for all your grandchildren. You are not their parents. You are not their source. You are definitely *not* the one who buys them what their parents have told them they cannot have, even if you bought it at Cracker Barrel.

While we must hold our extravagance in check where it is the most difficult to contain, which is with our perfect and sinless grandchildren, we must unleash it with others. Restaurant wait staff, for example. One waiter told me that waiters and waitresses hate working the lunch meal on Sunday. (By the way, I still use that word *waitress* because I'm over seventy-five. Also, by the way, I still use the words *actress* and *seamstress* and the phrase *master bedroom* because I will not be bullied.) The waiter said it was because all the church people, especially older church people, are very demanding, complain a lot, and tip little. The wait staff of a restaurant depend on tips. Tip generously. That is not the moment to count pennies. It's also not a moment to be rude and difficult to deal with. Why give the church a bad name? If you are going to be mean and leave a small tip, tell the waitress you are an atheist!

Keeping on giving as giving becomes more difficult and even scarier is one of the most powerful keys to living our senior years with joy. Giving with liberality rather than obligation is what makes generosity joyful. On the other hand, if you make giving all and only about giving money, you will lose the greater part. The life of generosity—true, free-hearted, openhanded generosity—opens the spout where the glory comes out.

Keep on giving freely. I do not mean merely financial giving, as important as that is. I mean giving everything good. Praise, affirmation, dessert, portions, tips, and compliments, especially compliments. One Sunday after I preached, an angry man confronted me in the lobby of the church. Did I say angry? Sorry. I did not mean to say angry. He was, as they say, "ripped out of the frame." He was so close to a stroke that he could hardly talk plain.

"Well, I'm finally leaving the church," he announced, sounding all the world like a teenage drama queen breaking up with her boyfriend. "I cannot attend a church where the pastor is a liar."

"What are you talking about?" I asked, feeling obligated to respond, even though his decision actually sounded good to me.

"I heard you. Maybe nobody else heard it, but I did. You talked about a WWI battle [which battle I can no longer remember], and you said it happened in 1917. I happen to be an expert in American military history. I know that battle did not happen until 1918. A man that would lie about a thing like that would lie about anything, and I cannot attend a church with a liar in the pulpit."

I said, "Well...bye."

I meant it. Adios. One can only imagine how many churches he has invaded, I mean attended, since then. How miserable he must be, wherever he goes to church, and how miserable his presence must make his pastor.

There was another man, however, in the same church, a lawyer, as remarkable as that may be, who was the most generous, affirming church member I've ever known. After every service, morning or night (yes, I said night service. We were Christians back then), he would tell me the same thing. "Pastor, that was the greatest sermon I've ever heard." Every time!

I was born at night, but I was not born last night. I know, at a cognitive level, that no one can preach the definitive homiletical masterpiece twice a week, week after week, for years. I know that in my mind, but I loved that lawyer for lying to me. When I came out of the pulpit, I was looking for that lawyer. Anyway, if you think of it correctly, in a way he was not lying. Mine was the best sermon he had heard at that particular service that precise morning. Right? I mean, isn't that right? He was not a lying lawyer. He was a generous man who gave and gave and kept on giving.

Here is a word to husbands about keeping on giving. When your wife walks out wearing that new dress she just bought at the mall, do not peer over the top of the sports page and growl, "How much did that set me back?" Or, "I'm going to confiscate your credit card." Or, "Who made that, Abdullah the Tent Maker?" Especially not that one. Ever.

Instead throw the paper aside and leap to your feet. "Oh, baby, look at you. You look like a million bucks in that dress! Wow! You wear that on Wednesday night and we are going to be late to prayer meeting."

A bit much, you say? I do not think so. She will love it. Think of all the compliments you gave her when she was young. Keep on giving.

My wife often tells me I am the handsomest, sexiest man she has ever seen. Pause a moment in your reading and look at my photo on the back of this book. Are we communicating? Obvious to all except those reading this in braille is that I am *not* the handsomest, sexiest man she has ever seen. Do not think for a moment that the ravages of age have stolen my sexy looks. I am not nor was I ever the handsomest, sexiest man she or anyone else ever saw. But her lies are music to my ears, as are mine to hers. Sweet and loving lies are the fabric of a generous senior's marriage.

Give and it shall be given unto you is not just an overused biblical quote to be used at the offering. It is a great truth. Generosity generates generosity. Giving unleashes giving, at any age. There is no reason to think that truth somehow melts as we age. Withholding likewise causes withholding. Young husbands and wives too cautious with their compliments and mutual affirmation grow even stingier as they age, and the marriage grows ever colder.

Some years ago I preached the funeral of a sweet Christian lady whose gruff and somewhat overly masculine husband had little use for the church. At the viewing he stood, as was the tradition, at the end of the casket, to acknowledge those who came to pay their respects. I was one of those, and when I approached I was amazed to see a stunning blanket of roses draped over the casket.

"Darrel," I said, "these roses are just gorgeous. I've never seen anything like this at a funeral."

"Well, I'll just tell you, Preacher. I paid for them roses myself. You know how Janet was. She was always wanting me to buy her roses and Valentine cards and such. I ain't into that mushy stuff, and I told her that. But I could see she was always kinda hurt. Well, I'm making it up to her now."

Really? At her funeral? I doubt she was blessed by his posthumous generosity. Give her the roses now! When you pull up to some inner-city street corner where a homeless guy is selling tiny rosebuds in plastic tubes, and she says, "Oh, buy me a rose," she does not want a bitter lecture on the socioeconomic implications of alcoholism. She just wants a rose. No, in fact, she just wants a reckless, romantic gesture from you. Just buy her the rose. No. Don't just buy her a rose. Call the vendor over and lower your window.

"Come here, my good man. My beautiful wife wants a rose, and I'm not going to buy her one. I'm going to buy all you've got."

Get loose. Get generous. Bless them both. Get your delighted sweetheart an armload of roses and a heart full of love.

Wives, don't wait to tell those at his funeral how wonderful he was. Tell him right now how wonderful he is. It doesn't matter if he is in his seventies and chubby and balding; tell him how handsome he is. Tell him he still rocks your world. Go on. Lie to him. Lie with persuasive energy and sparkling eyes. Lie with reckless abandon and with the knowledge that a generous, gracious, and loving God smiles on such sweet deceit. Lie to him knowing that the longer and more convincingly you assure him of his sexy good looks, the better he will look to you. The heart of the matter is the matter of the heart.

I heard the late great Billy Graham tell a group of preachers about an experience he had trying to carefully manage the tension between one Sunday morning's offering and the eyes of onlookers. He said he and his wife, Ruth, were attending a tiny Southern Baptist church as guests. He was not there to preach, but one can imagine the impact of the famous preacher's presence. He knew everyone in the little church was watching his every move.

As the offering plate approached, Graham reached into his pocket for a ten-dollar bill which he remembered was among several twenties. He pulled out a twenty by accident; but he did not want the whole church to see him swap it for a smaller bill, so he donated the accidental twenty. In the car on the way home he told his wife, "I guess we will get a bigger blessing than I intended. I reached for a ten and came out with a twenty. I knew everyone was watching so I just gave the twenty."

"Oh, no, Billy," Ruth said. "We still only get a ten-dollar blessing. In your heart that twenty was a ten."

I don't know how Graham felt. Personally, I hate it when God speaks to me through members of my family, especially my wife!

Some seniors may say, oh, no, I cannot be generous. I am on a fixed income. Generosity is not about amount but attitude. A person on Social Security can give a small amount and actually be generous. Likewise, a billionaire can give a large amount and be cheap.

In the New Testament, Jesus praised the generosity of a poor widow (one may assume she was an elderly widow) who gave only two small coins. He admired her not because of how much she gave but for how freely she gave. In the previous chapter a nurse's aide eloquently stated, "Old don't gotta mean mean." In the story of the widow's mite Jesus was making another great point that is well taken: Old don't gotta mean cheap.

CHAPTER 7
KEEP ON KEEPING IT REAL

Stupidity is also a gift of God,
but one mustn't misuse it.
—POPE JOHN PAUL II

T HE STORY IS told that in the depths of the Great Depression, an Iowa farmer, desperate to save the family farm, resorted to applying for a job with a passing circus. Seeing the help-wanted sign, the farmer applied at the manager's wagon without any real hope of being hired. He had tried for many other jobs and was never hired. He found to his amazement that the manager hired him on the spot, no questions asked, no interview, and no application. Now the farmer was suspicious.

"What is the job?" the farmer asked.

"Oh, you'll like it," the manager said. "And the pay is good. Real good."

"What do I have to do?"

"Here's the situation," the manager finally confessed. "Our gorilla died, and his act was the most popular in the whole circus. With this Depression on we cannot afford to get another one from Africa. What we could do, however, is skin him out. All you have to do is put on the gorilla suit and pretend to be the gorilla. It's easy. Big strong guy like you. You'll be great, and the animal trainer will teach you how."

Conservative, shy, and taciturn, the big farmer had no interest in being a gorilla or any other animal for that matter, but he was desperate. He could not lose the family farm. He humbled himself, joined the circus, and learned to mimic the gorilla's moves.

The act was fairly simple but exciting to watch. Every night the massive African primate would swing out over the lion's cage on a carefully measured rope. It infuriated the lion, which would leap up at the gorilla in futility and roar ferociously in his rage and frustration. The audiences went wild, and to his amazement the farmer liked it. The people would cheer and applaud wildly and throw bananas. No one had ever before cheered for him or applauded or thought him in the least entertaining. As reluctant as he had been to accept the strange job, the farmer now found himself in the most thrilling job of his life.

One night he decided to make the act even more exciting. He carried a rolled-up newspaper in his paw as he swung out over the lion's cage. When the enraged beast leaped up at him the gorilla hit the lion across the nose; but as he did, the farmer quite forgot himself and let go of the rope with the other hand. When he landed in the cage, the king of the jungle was on him in a flash. With one frightening paw on each of the gorilla's shoulders, the lion opened his huge mouth inches from the horrified farmer's face and roared.

The terrifying sound was deafening, and the farmer screamed, "Help me! Somebody get me out of here. Please, please, help me!"

"Shut up, you fool," the lion whispered. "You're going to get us both fired."

Monkey suit living is not living at all. It's pretend, the imitation of life, the loss of who we are in an impotent pursuit of what we cannot become. Such a futile existence is never very attractive. As we age it becomes sad and even ridiculous. Nothing is more tedious than a seventy-year-old man who still wants to recount his glory days playing high school football. It's over, and he is the only one who does not know that. No one, absolutely no one, is impressed anymore if they ever were. Somebody needs to tell him. Let it go! Move on. You cannot ever again be who you were at seventeen, and perhaps you were never as great as you thought you were. And, anyway, guess what? It is over.

The seventy-ish woman who dresses like a twenty-ish ingenue is just plain embarrassing-ish. Somebody needs to tell her she does not have to wear "old woman" clothes. Indeed, she shouldn't! But the alternative is not looking laughable in clothes her granddaughter just might wear. There is a way to dress appropriately that signals to the world she knows how old she is and is determined to look nice—*for her age*—without wearing her denial like a laughable monkey suit.

Different stages of aging have different physical attractiveness goals. One goal, which is attainable through much of one's later years, is to be a "great-fer." The other, which follows when that one is no longer as possible as it once was, is to be a "good-fer."

Goal one is to hear that your neighbors say about you, "She (he) looks great-fer her (his) age."

Then comes, "She (he) looks good-fer her (his) age."

For a good part of the journey into aging, one can still be a great-fer. Later one can accept being at the good-fer stage.

What one never wants is to get stranded at the "who does she (he) think she's (he's) fooling" stage. Great-fers and good-fers are attractive and genuine and bespeak a calm self-awareness that is nonetheless determined to look "great fer" or at least "good fer" one's age as long as possible.

What you are about to read next must be said, and, let's be honest, some of you now reading this book *need* to hear it. Being old need not mean dressing like you've lost all self-respect. Utterly ridiculous is the sight of an elderly man in Bermuda shorts, an Alpine fedora with a perky little feather in the brim, high-top black socks, and dress shoes. There is simply no excuse for that. Out for a walk you don't have to dress like George Clooney at a Hollywood party, but Bermuda shorts and high-top black socks? No. Just *no*. Get those pathetic duds out of your closet. And keep them out. Now and forever. Keeping on keeping it real means being who you are, but it also means not violating the fundamental laws of civilized society. Keeping it real does not mean keeping it ludicrous.

The issue is authenticity not eccentricity, and the key to authenticity is being honest with ourselves. Of course, that is true at any age, but it is especially important as we age. Facing facts is just plain tough to do, but face them we must. I remember the exact moment when I knew I looked old to young people. I had preached the evening service for a very young pastor in Alabama, and his wife and I started down the back steps together when she reached her hand out to take my arm. I realized it was a spontaneous gesture of genuine concern. She was steadying the old guy on the dark stairs, and it was a bit of a shock.

One can do two things in moments such as that. One is to jerk your arm away from such a silly young woman confused enough to think you need help on the stairs. Or you can humble yourself and thank God somebody cares enough to prevent you from breaking your hip. There are different seasons of life. To cling to one that is obviously, manifestly *over* will make us look ridiculous.

Turn the page. Embrace the journey. It is OK not to be as young as you once were and not to look as young as you once did. It is OK to hold the handrails on the escalator. Holding the handrails does not make you old. Staying alive did that. Holding the handrail makes you smart. It is OK to use ear plugs when the music is too loud. It is also OK to wear a hearing aid when voices are too soft. And, by the way, whatever happened to everybody speaking up? When did the whole world decide it was good to whisper all the time? It is not wearing hearing aids that makes seniors seem old. What makes us seem old is refusing to wear them and constantly asking everyone to repeat everything.

Never turn down a helping hand. It is prideful and dangerous. The Bible is clear on this. "Pride goes before a broken hip." I'm pretty sure that's in there somewhere. Keeping it real means being real about what aging means without being a victim of it. Recently after giving a speech I found myself about to jump down from the stage. It was not a height suitable for paragliding. It was just a couple of feet to the main floor. Yet discretion proved the better part of valor, and I walked down to the stairs at the end of the stage. That is not victimhood, and it is not cowardice. It is keeping it real.

"Age is just a number" is something young people tell themselves so they won't be afraid of the future. Age is not just a number. It actually correlates to how old the body is that I walk around in. It is real. It indicates real changes in that body, especially my joints and my sleep pattern and how much I eat, and sometimes it indicates something else. What was it? Oh, right. My memory. No. It is not just a number.

I do not have to surrender without a fight, but I do have to keep it real. I do not look like I did at twenty-five. I cannot play church league basketball as I did then. I cannot go out to eat at midnight, eat a side of beef and an entire cheesecake, sleep quietly without indigestion, and get up the next morning hoping to do it again. That is not a mere number. That is my current reality, but it does not destroy my happiness or make my life meaningless.

To everything there is a season. A time for playing basketball and a time for watching basketball. A time for all-nighters and a time for afternoon naps. I *know* that's in the Bible. At least that is what it meant.

Our son is the pastor of a substantial church in Georgia which, of course, my wife and I attend when I am not on the road. We enjoy arriving early to spend lots of time out in the lobby meeting and greeting. I consider myself the unofficial public relations director for my son and his church. I love to joke with the teenagers and tell them how good-looking they are or ask them about school or their life goals. When the youth pastor resigned, several of the teens asked our son, Pastor Travis, if I could be the new youth pastor. It was one of the greatest honors of my life. Of course, I would not last a week. One lock-in and I would be in the ICU. Then again, maybe...well, no.

On the other hand, the youth pastor probably could not serve as an executive-level management consultant for colleges, businesses, and churches. We seniors have to know who we are and who we no longer are, what we can do and what we can no longer do, even if we ever really could. It's painful to keep in mind that not everything included in our personal mythology actually happened as we remember it.

Ever hear an older man watching a college football game say, "I could still do better than that"? Actually, no, he couldn't. He could not even live over one practice. He could not run the length of the field. He could never deal with one night in the athletic dorm, and his wife could not be a cheerleader. The thing is, that is all OK. One man told me he played football in high school but not in college. I asked him if, looking back on it now, he thought he could have made it at the college level?

"Now?" he asked. "Oh, sure, now I do. I was just barely on the first team in high school, but the older I get the better I was." Such an honest sense of humor is rare and winsome. We must be OK with who we are now, in this season of life, and rejoice in the youth we watch play the sports and accomplish in life what is no longer ours to do.

Do you ever look in the mirror and for a fleeting second you cannot think who that old person is? Then suddenly the truth explodes in your face. *Oh, no!* That is me. That is the reality with which we must come to terms. That person is not a younger you in disguise. That is you now. As rugged a discipline as it is, we must keep on keeping it real.

I once heard the story of an eighty-year-old man who was out for a stroll when a frog hopped out into the path. The frog spoke to him in a lovely female voice.

"I am a beautiful princess under a witch's spell. She turned me into a frog, and I must remain one until a man kisses me. I beg of you," said the frog, "kiss me and break the spell. If you will just kiss me, I will turn back into a princess, and I promise I will be yours."

The old man picked up the frog, put it in his pocket, and walked on to the house of his friend, who was also in his eighties. Once there he showed the little green creature to his elderly friend.

"Look what I found," he said, holding the frog in the palm of his hand.

The frog repeated its story. "Look, I'm telling you the truth. I am not really a frog. I am a beautiful princess under the spell of a cruel witch. If you will kiss me, the spell will be broken. I will turn back into a princess, and I will be all yours."

His friend said, "Go on. Kiss it. What can it hurt? Maybe it's telling the truth. Go on and kiss it."

"No," said the old man as he pocketed the frog. "At this stage of my life I'd rather have a talking frog."

Admitting I'm no longer in my twenties is not admitting defeat. It is keeping it real. At any stage of life, we do better to face facts, especially about ourselves. I played high school football. In my freshman year I got a chance to actually enter a game. We were so far behind that the coach was reluctant to endanger the life of anybody good. I was a ninth grader playing free safety and determined to show that I could play with the big boys. The other team had a senior running back, a local legend who later went on to play college football. On one play he broke through our linebackers and was running diagonally across right in front of me.

This was my chance. I lowered my head and charged. I was about to stick my helmet right in this star's ribs, and my coach would see how good I was. This was certainly my chance. My last thought was, yeah, he doesn't even see me coming.

When I came to I was looking up at the stadium lights and thought I could hear laughter from both sets of stands. He changed direction so fast and hit me so hard that for a few seconds I could not even think where I was. Lying there on my back trying to come fully awake, however, I did know one thing. I was never going to play for the Dallas Cowboys.

That was one hard-hitting dose of reality, and I have found since then that reality often hits like a freight train. Living in denial is not necessarily faith, and it is not necessarily keeping your dream alive. It may just be keeping a nightmare alive for everybody around you.

❧

At one small church we attended for a while there was a family singing group whose last name was Talent—hence their stage name, The Five Talents. There were, in fact, five of them, but not a single talent was among them. They were quite frankly talentless at a painful level. They evidently did not know this. They wanted to sing occasionally, and the pastor would not tell them no. They should never have called themselves The Five Talents. I know it was their family name, but it only added to the snickering, embarrassing pain. They were not the five talents. They were not even The Three Talents and Two Who Are Marginal. They were horrible. Fingernails on a blackboard horrible.

They scarred me for life. I have this paranoid fear of being in denial about something I am attempting to do. I am sickened at the very thought of some group meeting secretly drawing straws for who has to tell me I am no good at it. The problem of The Five Talents is always the same. No one will tell the truth to folks like the Talents. No one has the nerve to say, "Look, you guys are wonderful people. We all love you, but you have to hear this. You cannot sing on this platform anymore. No. Just plain no. We need ushers and greeters. We are way short of parking lot workers. But singing? No. That's finished." Here's a law of leadership. To protect everyone else and the event itself, somebody has to tell the Talents.

Many years ago Alison and I took the children to see a small theater production of *Camelot*, a musical we dearly love. What made the experience memorable but unenjoyable was the actress playing Guinevere. She was way too long in the tooth for the Guinevere role, easily fifty years of age and fifty pounds overweight. She looked like King Arthur's mother. The best explanation I could come up with was that her husband was a Mafia don to whom the theater was in debt. I was mortified, which is hard to explain. Why should I have been embarrassed? I never understand that about myself. Things like Guinevere and The Five Talents always make me feel embarrassed.

I still travel. I still lecture and preach frequently, but I am determined to know when to hang up my spurs. Right now I can still do the job, but at seventy-six I am not a kid anymore. I extracted a promise from my sweet wife, hand over her heart and hope to die. The minute I start saying goofy stuff on the platform and don't seem to know what city I'm in, tell me! Please do not let me end my ministry as a sad Alzheimer's joke. Platform ministry is over at that point, and I suppose there is nothing left to do but run for president.

I met with the board of a small church in Alabama. Their pastor of sixty-three years was now nearing ninety years of age and frankly could not do it anymore. He had been in and out of the hospital for several years. He looked pathetic, and his poor little wife was a frail, empty shell. His board was asking him to retire, but he had dug in his heels. They brought me in to see if I could help.

"Retirement is not in the Bible," the pastor said.

I said, "Neither is gall bladder surgery, Pastor, and you had that last year."

The board and I were talking to a brick wall. He was never going to step down. Never. The little church loved him and could not bring themselves to force the issue. Meanwhile the church was dying at about the same speed he was.

The issue, it turned out, was something of a fantasy he had. He wanted to "die with his boots on," as he put it. He imagined going down swinging, preaching his last message and dropping dead in the pulpit. It was pure melodrama, and it was pride. What a sad story. He was a man who had served the God of ultimate reality his whole life and now refused to face reality at the end of his life.

Keeping it real means being in touch with where we are in life. I suppose notable exceptions happen, but on the whole there comes a moment when we have done the deal, at least most of the deal.

Accepting that and looking back with gratitude on where we have been and what has been accomplished is not weak resignation. It is called contentment.

Our son is a fine pastor and a brilliant preacher. Today as I write this, I can still go pretty hard. I am still getting more invitations than I can accept. But when this season of my life is finished, I'm not going to turn into The Five Talents. I am already rehearsing for my next job, and when it's time I'll be ready to do it. I have been the pastor. My next job will be the pastor's father. It will not mean I've failed or given up or quit too soon. It will mean I have been promoted, and I will do that job until I get one final promotion.

CHAPTER 8

KEEP ON FORGIVING

Sometimes the first step to forgiveness is understanding the other person is a complete idiot.

—ANONYMOUS

ONE OF MY favorite stories is that of a man who was a deer hunter, an inveterate deer hunter. He never missed an opening day, and every year he begged his wife to go with him. Hunting, he said, was something they could do together. He offered to get her a rifle and teach her everything, but every year she declined, shocked that he would even suggest such a thing.

Finally she decided he was right. Furthermore she decided to surprise him. She secretly bought a beautiful Savage Arms 110 bolt-action rifle and enough ammunition for a small militia. At the salesman's recommendation she also took shooting lessons, at which she discovered, to her shock, that she was a natural shot. She and her instructor were amazed at her incredible accuracy. She proudly took the rifle home to surprise her hunter husband.

He was surprised, to say the least, and genuinely overjoyed. He had dreamed of this. Likewise he was delighted with her choice of rifles; but, of course, he wanted to know if she knew how to use the expensive weapon.

"Just let me demonstrate," she responded triumphantly, at which they went into a field near their home. When she began to shoot the walnuts off the trees, all doubt was removed from the husband's mind. This was great. This was an answer to his prayers. At last he had a wife who wanted to go hunting with him and who could shoot like Annie Oakley.

The opening day of deer season he took her to a likely stretch of woods where he had hunted in the past. Leaving her in a deer stand, he explained that he would circle around the hills ahead and see if one would run toward her.

"If I hear you shoot," he assured her, "I will come back immediately."

He had hardly gotten out of sight, however, when he heard the report of her rifle. Jogging back to the stand where he'd left her, he found her holding the rifle on a terrified man, hands raised, backed up to a pine tree and shivering in his boots.

"What in the world is going on here?" demanded the shocked husband.

"I have killed this deer," she explained, "and this man is trying to drag him off."

"No, lady," said the frightened man. "You can have the deer. Just let me get my saddle off of him."

The kind of legalistic reductionism which hopes to make life work by memorizing laws can backfire. One can learn all the "rules" for successful living and wind up skillfully killing the wrong animal. "Just tell me the rules" may work in physics, but it does not work in relationships. People are not machines. Treat your spouse like a ballistic galvanometer, whatever that is, and find out. Of all relationships marriage is the least mechanical. Of all seasons in marriage the senior years are the most emotionally complex and sensitive.

Some of the glue that held it together in the early years may have lost its adhesiveness. Just as our bodies tend to get more brittle and less resilient, our emotions can lose their elasticity. Anger can be closer to the surface. Old, unresolved hurts now leave sensitive places with raw nerve endings that others can touch unintentionally. Those painful jolts of electricity may have always been there, but as we age they become harder to hide. Harder or perhaps we just do not try as hard to hide them. Perhaps, we figure, that hurt. It hurt a lot, and I'm old; and I deserve to show it hurt. In fact, I deserve to hurt somebody back.

That is the point where all the rules fail us. It is why I never liked that WWJD idea. What would Jesus do? Why does that help me? I know very well what Jesus would do. Walk on water. Feed the five thousand. I *know* what He would do. I know the rules. I learned them in Vacation Bible School. It's just that the rules seem far away and unhelpful because everything has changed, and it makes me feel confused and uncertain and insecure when a bank clerk younger than my children is condescending and rude to me just because I do not *want* to do online banking. I want a checkbook, a real paper checkbook with a register that one writes in with a ballpoint pen. And why should that be so hard to get? And thank you very much.

Memorized rules will not help in that tense moment at that desk in that bank office. I need to live in the flow of forgiveness, or like the lady deer hunter I may confuse the bank officer with the crazy computerized world that seems determined to expose my every insecurity. Anyway, how can he be an "officer" at an age when he should be bagging groceries after school? How old is he anyway? Seventeen?

What helps? The only thing that helps is to keep on bathing in an unceasing stream of forgiveness.

As we age we tend to want it to be right. And by right we mean the way it used to be. They used to give you a free toaster when you opened an account here. Whatever happened to *that*? We have to get it through our old gray (or bald) heads. It will never be right again. I cannot make it right or argue it right ever again. That train has left the station. And it is *not* coming back.

If I live in the changed world angry that it has changed, I give it power over me. Now I am not only aging; I am aging and defeated. Over and over again. I am defeated every time I let my cell phone buffalo me into an angry explosion. I am defeated every time I get angry because my waitress has an incredibly and nauseatingly pierced tongue. OK. Let's be honest. That is "dith-guthting." But why exactly does it make me angry? Because waitresses never used to have pierced tongues and the world in which that is OK and even common is frightening to me. And fear makes me angry.

If I can live and walk in forgiveness, if forgiveness flows up inside me like a spring, it will flow out of me and over those frightening people and things around me. Forgiveness, like love, is not all about feeling. It is a life decision. I can decide to be a forgiving person, and because that decision is mine it means I am in control. I am not the defeated, frightened elderly victim of this crazy new world and the teenagers who run it. I decided. I am in control because nothing and no one can make me not forgive it, him, her, the bank, the waitress, whatever.

Dealing with that insolent child who runs the bank is one thing. Those closest to me are another. Friction is increased by several factors. Two of those are roughness and proximity. In other words, the more things (people) rub against each other and the rougher they are, the more friction they create. Hello! That sounds like two married seniors in the same dwelling.

The friction in a seniors' marriage can be considerably increased by factors that were entirely predictable, except we ignored them. Again, a self-granted exemption. Other older married couples may experience increased friction…but *we* will not because we are different, better, in fact, than all the rest of those couples. The question is fairly simple, and the answer is obvious. If two unfinished human beings that have not spent huge amounts of daily life together suddenly spend basically all day every day together, perhaps in a smaller space than they enjoyed for the previous fifty years, would that increase friction? Duh. Now retired, they do not come home to each other; they are home *with* each other. All the time. All day. Every day. Which is why "downsizing" too early may not be the panacea everyone says it is. It will predictably increase friction, and friction causes heat and maybe even fire.

Another factor that can increase the friction is that the more confined space can be seen as "belonging" to one spouse and not the other, at least not as much. Seniors have tended to have a more traditional marriage in that the house and its work were seen as "hers" and work outside the home and being the principal wage earner were more "his," even if they both had jobs. Now he is retired, and unstated expectations can seriously increase the friction. She has always dreamed that when he or they both retire they would joyfully share the household chores and yard work in a beautiful new and very Hallmark way. In reality he may try to do the housework stuff, but it's new to him. Also he may find it feels as if he, who has been somebody's boss, now has a boss. Her. He has suddenly gone to work for her doing unfamiliar tasks her way. Friction.

Or his unstated expectation all the years of his career may have been that in retirement she would keep doing all the housework and he would trade work for golf. In that imagined scenario she may very well feel that retirement has changed everything for him and nothing for her. He may assume she will still cook as she always did when the kids were around. She may assume she will never cook again. The underlying issue is that for decades of marriage they never discussed what retirement should look like. Highly predictable friction totally unpredicted makes for a disappointing shock to both spouses.

At least part of the answer is time apart. He may golf or go fishing or start to build model trains or do the yard work he always resisted in the past. She may suddenly start to volunteer at the local food bank or join a garden club in which she has shown no interest in the past. The unstated and perhaps subconscious purpose of both is not just the fishing or the study of chrysanthemums. It's time apart. As we age, our marriages need to create the time apart that life's realities provided in our younger years. Some well-planned and agreed-upon time alone and apart beats sniping at each other all day.

You finally have all the kids out of the house. They're all married and raising their own children and doing their own stuff. Even the last one. The slow-to-launch one is finally out of the basement. Yay! The house is paid for and even better than that; it's empty. First, you celebrate. You take a cruise or buy a camper. Great. That euphoria lasts, what—two months? Then what? You face the sobering reality that you two are alone in the house. Well, not exactly alone. You are with each other and no kids are watching. This is the moment for some rethinking. All the things you never talked about during all the years you should have talked about them now need to be talked about.

Should he get a part-time job? Should she? Should they move to Florida like everyone else they know. Are there any people over seventy left in Michigan? What about volunteering? What about tutoring kids at a local school?

The question is biblical. How then shall we live?

Our senior years should be great years. Right? How do we make them great? He may have to pitch in around the house and take on doing some things he never used to do. She may have to let him do those things in his own way which may very well be a poorer way or even a stupid way. Let him do it. Let him fold clothes in some weird way and put the socks away by tossing them like tiny basketballs into an open drawer. The clothes are still folded, and some of the socks may actually land in the drawer. If she cannot stand to watch, she should leave the room.

Likewise, a senior husband whose ego is so fragile he cannot take a suggestion from his wife has managed somehow to make it through decades of bumps and bruises tragically unhelped by any of it. By the time he reaches his senior years a male ought to have come up against the devastating truth that he does not know everything and the even harsher reality that his wife may know lots more than he thought.

The wise senior husband finds a delightful moment discovering new dimensions in the person to whom he has been married all these years. She may be much more capable and intelligent and insightful than he realized. If he is a real man, this is exciting. If he is fragile and defensive, he will turn what might have been a fun new season of life into a long, painful day in a dentist's chair just trying to grip the arms till the drilling finally stops.

Women live their whole married lives under the misguided belief they are married to an adult. Nonsense. Men do not grow up. They just get big. As men get older and heavier and slower it makes them appear even more grown. Get that out of your head, lady. You are now married to an older, slower, heavier, arthritic, balding twelve-year-old. He needs, not wants, *needs* to shoot free throws with those socks and pretend he is Larry Byrd. Much has changed physically since you married him. Nothing has changed mentally.

And you, sir. Nobody gets to marry a photograph. Everybody marries a movie. You cannot marry a teenage girl, stay married fifty years, give her four babies, and expect her not to spread out. That is unreasonable. In one counseling session a late fifties man with male pattern baldness and an over-the-belt paunch complained that his wife just did not turn him on anymore. He either was or pretended to be shocked when I pointed out to him that he wasn't exactly Tom Cruise.

She needed compliments when she was young. She needed to hear how beautiful she was. And how much you loved her. Nothing has changed. She still needs it. Why does she watch the Hallmark movies? They all have the same plot and the same actors, and they're all filmed at the same quaint mountain lodge in Vermont. She watches them for the same reason you pretend to be Arnold Palmer when you're golfing. She still needs a touch of romance in her life. She doesn't just want compliments and kisses. She *needs* them.

We are in this together. Young together, old together. You courted her in her twenties. Court her in her seventies.

The story is told of an older couple who came in for marriage counseling with their young pastor. After listening to them the pastor spoke frankly to the husband. "What she wants from you is affection. Do you understand? Regular, sincere affection. Get it?"

"No," said the husband, "I don't."

After trying for some time to explain it to the older man, the frustrated young pastor decided to demonstrate. He took the wife, a woman his mother's age, in his arms and kissed her passionately.

"There," said the pastor, "like that. Just like that. She needs that every day."

"Well, every day would be a real challenge for me, Pastor, but I could bring her in three days a week."

Forgiveness is about release. Release each other to be older, heavier, and slower. Release each other to be apart some. Lots maybe. Release each other not to be what you expected. Release life itself not to be exactly what you expected. When we hold others in bondage to our expectations we only make ourselves miserable, and we effect no change whatsoever in them.

There are two kinds of people. Only two. Those who wear huge sombreros in the airport on the way home from Mexico and mouse ears on the way home from Disney World. And those who do not. Neither is right. Neither is wrong. They are both who they are, and both are being true to themselves. They just do not understand each other. They live in the same universe, but that's about the extent of the similarity. Perhaps they work together. They have to travel together professionally, but deep inside they can hardly tolerate each other. They do not even know that the line of demarcation is the sombrero.

They stare at each other and wonder what is wrong with this guy.

The mouse ears guy is having the time of his life. Hey, isn't this great? Everybody in the airport is looking at me. The non-ears fellow is mortified. He would not be caught dead wearing mouse ears all alone in the privacy of his own house. He thinks to himself that if the angels are watching he does not want them to see him in a stupid sombrero with a donkey and the word *Guadalajara* stitched on the brim. They tolerate each other. Their jobs demand it, but they could never vacation together. They are cordial, but that is the extent of it. They cannot really be friends. If they try, it will be only minutes before one says, "Hey, don't touch my mouse ears." To which the other will respond, "Either take them off or go in the other room. It embarrasses me just to look at you."

They are both good guys. They both know the rules. Love your neighbor. Somehow, something is missing; and the older they get, the more the ragged edge of whatever is missing grates on both sets of nerves. Unless they release each other—forgive each other's sombrero/non-sombrero, mouse ear/non-mouse ear differences—they can never really connect. Underneath their forced proximity will be a simmering anger that will disallow anything close to love.

Do you remember that incredible Howard Beale scene in the film *Network*? The TV anchorman, Howard Beale (played by Peter Finch), tells his viewers to go to the window and shout how angry they are, in no uncertain terms. I suggest a different approach. Start releasing others. Things. Circumstances. Life. Your spouse and your grown kids and your grandkids. Start saying to Washington, DC, and its corruption and lying and dementia...I release you. Go out in the parking lot of the DMV or the bank and say, I release you. Look up at the sky and say, I release you. I release you to be different. To fail. To be stupid. To disappoint me. I release you. And in that release I can love again.

While I served as the president of a certain university, a father of one of the students came to see me. With thousands of students on campus I could not possibly know all of them, but I happened to know his son.

"Oh, I know your son," I told him. "What a fine young man. He is a real leader on this campus. You must be very proud of him."

He brushed my praise off like dust. "Yeah, yeah. I know all that. That is not why I'm here."

"Why are you here?" I asked, more than a little shocked.

"It's that earring. I can't stand that thing. Every time I look at him I can't see anything but that earring. I've told him a thousand times, and he's still wearing it."

I tried to make my voice as soothing as possible. But seeing his expression and hearing the tone of his voice, I really knew it would do no good. "Look, your son is a fine young man with a great future. Perhaps that earring..."

"Perhaps nothing. I want you to make him take it out. Do you understand? When he comes home for Thanksgiving, I want that earring gone or I will pull him out of this school."

I wanted to say, "Look, sir, you've had him for twenty years. I've had him for three semesters. Why is it my job?" That's what I wanted to say, but I sensed intuitively he was not going to be open to that line of reasoning. The next day I called his son into my office.

"Do you know who was in my office yesterday?"

"Yes, sir," he answered, "and I know why. He wants you to make me ditch the earring."

"Son," I said. "Your dad is a piece of work."

"Oh, Dr. Rutland, he is driving me crazy over this earring. It's all he talks about. He's letting it ruin our relationship. Over an earring! Isn't that stupid?"

"It is stupid," I agreed. "Imagine letting something as stupid as an earring stand between you and someone you love."

"I know," he said.

"Think of it. An earring? That is selfish. He is letting an earring endanger a relationship as important as yours. How can he do that?" I said.

"Exactly!" the young man said. "Exactly! It is selfish. How can anybody be that...Oh, I know what you're doing."

"Look, son," I said. "One of you is going to have to be an adult. And I met your dad."

The light dawned. I could see it in his eyes. He looked like John Belushi in the back of James Brown's church. "You're right," he said. "I never thought about it that way. I made it all about him. It's about me too, isn't it?"

I've never been so proud of a student in my life. He took that earring out and laid it on my coffee table like he was an old wino in a Bowery mission swearing off liquor. "My father will never see that earring again."

I am in my seventies. I do not really like seeing males wear earrings. To me, like the bride with a dragon tattoo, they look like pirates. Or worse. Personally I think they should give all their earrings to their sisters. On the other hand, how big a deal is it? As we age and the cultural trappings around us shift, we must decide what is really important to us. Is it the earring, or is it our relationship with the person who wears it? I am not suggesting we compromise morally just because we have aged a bit. We do not have to endorse the wickedness of others but must not let trivialities destroy what is or ought to be most valuable to us.

When your grandchild comes home wearing a tattoo of a dragon, you will have some choices to make and you will have to make them fast. You can blow up and let the collateral damage happen as it will. You can do that. I warn you though. That explosion may be more destructive for much longer than you expect and the stray shrapnel may hit where you did not expect it.

Keeping on forgiving means, in part at least, letting molehills stay molehills. It means releasing folks you love, and those you don't, for that matter, to have opinions different from yours, wear clothes you hate, and make stupid career moves you can see are stupid and evidently they cannot. Let go. Let them do stupid stuff and be ready to catch them when they fall. If it is as stupid as you think it is, when their parents get finished explaining exactly how stupid it was and when they face the consequences of said stupidity, they will need loving, understanding grandparents when it blows up in their sweet little faces.

I was preaching in a very traditional Holiness church one Sunday when I witnessed an amazing thing. In that church the pastor and I sat in chairs on the platform, from which I could see all the way to the back. In the middle of the song service a teenage boy who had quite obviously never been there before wandered in. His jeans were dangerously low on his hips. His multicolored hair was spiked, and the tats on his arms were massive. He looked confused as if uncertain where he was or how he had gotten there.

I saw an elderly woman leave her pew and approach the boy. I thought, oh, no, she is going to run this kid off before he can say sanctified holy. I vastly underestimated the old saint. I watched her put her arm around him and guide him into her pew. She held her hymnbook (yes, I said hymnbook; I told you it was a traditional church) and guided his eyes down the verses with her old finger. They smiled at each other, and he stayed for my sermon.

Afterward I saw her and asked if the boy was her grandson. "No," she said. "I've never seen him before. He isn't my grandson, but he's somebody's grandson."

None of the rules she had learned in Sunday school helped her in that complex cross-cultural collision. A formula couldn't help her at that human intersection. She released him. Forgave him, if you will, and whatever she felt, it felt like love to him. She is gone now. That was many years ago. I was young then so she seemed very old to me. She was probably younger than I am now. I remember her plain black dress and the no-nonsense bun on the back of her head. I know make-up had never touched her face. I also remember her gentle smile and her kindness to a strange boy who could not have been any more different from her.

One of my favorite sayings has been couched in different words and variously attributed to folks from the ancient Greeks to Ashley Montagu. My own paraphrase is "the goal of life is to die young, as old as possible." I observed that remarkable scene with the elderly woman in that oh-so-traditional Holiness church in the 1980s, some forty years ago. She must have died many years ago. I know nothing about her, not even her name, but I do know this. She was a kind old lady, very kind and very old, who died very young.

CHAPTER 9
KEEP ON BEING GRATEFUL

I feel a very unusual sensation—
if it is not indigestion, I think
it must be gratitude.
—BENJAMIN DISRAELI

I F THERE IS one complaint seniors consistently voice against young people it is that they feel entitled. Perhaps that accusation is valid. Perhaps not. If it is, it is also the subject of another book to be written by somebody else. This book is for us about us and written by one of us seniors. As irritating as entitled Gen-Xers can be, nothing grates on the nerves of society quite like a sullen, entitled senior citizen filled with self-pity.

In one church I pastored were two elderly sisters. They proved to me that DNA is not the determinant many think it is. Ethel and Myrtle could not have been any less alike, physically and emotionally. They were both in their early seventies, both attended my church, and both were childless widows. Beyond that they were not from the same tribe or galaxy.

Myrtle was the slightly younger and far more prosperous of the two. Her husband's insurance policy and considerable estate had left her well cared for with a beautiful debt-free home and regular income. She also drove a luxury car and dressed well. Yet she was the most negative, pessimistic, self-absorbed human being I have ever met.

Nothing was ever right. Nothing. I could greet her with good morning at the door of the church, and she would launch into a dozen reasons why it was *not* a good morning and why she did not appreciate my claiming it was. In fact, she hated the phrase "Good morning" because it assumed others were all bright and cheery when in fact they were lonely and in pain and upset because the night before had not gone well and the morning was not starting well and did not hold promise of being good. Not in the least. She had not slept well the night before. She never slept well, and furthermore I should know this—evidently because she had informed me of it in the past, and anyway, what kind of pastor cannot remember the serious problems of his people?

She was exhausting. So much so that I dreaded seeing her. When I saw her Caddy enter the church parking lot, I suddenly found I had left something in my office that I needed immediately.

Ethel, the older and poorer of the two sisters, was a sweet and memorable blessing in my life. She had married a longshoreman in her teens and left Georgia to follow him to California. One can only assume this was to get away from her sister. In his late sixties her husband had been killed in a work-place accident and left her nothing. She returned to Georgia penniless and arthritic, to be near her only family, her irascible younger sister. She did not share the large comfortable home with Myrtle. I doubt if Myrtle had offered such an arrangement, but if she had only a masochist would have accepted. Instead Ethel lived in a crime-ridden government housing complex in a nearby town.

She could not be at my church, her home church, very often because it required someone to drive the forty-five minutes each way. When she came, however, she was a blessing. She enjoyed every minute of the service, especially my sermon, which only served to prove that she was a wise and discerning woman. Of course.

I would visit her at her apartment occasionally, always in broad daylight. The police were probably called to that complex more than all other areas of the town combined. Not only did Ethel not complain, she seemed totally content to live there. In fact, I never heard her complain about anything including her sister, about whom I complained to God on a regular basis.

One afternoon I went to visit Ethel, but she did not answer her door. I decided to try the back door. Hers was a ground floor apartment with a little concrete back "porch" so called. It was only big enough for one chair, but I knew Ethel sat back there sometimes. As I rounded the corner of the building I could hear her singing. She was snapping green beans into a large basin on her lap and singing an old hymn. I could see that her little arthritic hands could hardly do what she was asking of them, and she winced ever so slightly with each effort. She did not see me, but I could see her and hear what she was singing.

> Count your blessings, name them one by
> one;
> Count your blessings, see what God hath
> done.[1]

As I left my observation post and greeted Ethel, I wondered what blessings were hers to count.

"Hello, Miss Ethel. How are you today?"

"Oh, hello, Preacher. What a nice surprise!"

"It's nice to see you too. I heard you singing."

"Oh, no!" she wailed in mock horror. "I can't believe you sneaked up on me and heard my croaky old voice."

"I love to hear you sing. But I do have one question. You seem really happy today. What particular blessings are you counting today?"

"Oh!" She gushed like a teenage girl the day of her prom. "This is a wonderful day. The young woman who lives above me had a baby. She and the baby are coming home today, and I'm making supper for her family. Isn't that exciting? A new baby in our building! And I had enough extra this month to pay for their supper. That is today's blessing. Isn't God wonderful?"

Miss Ethel had plenty to be angry about. More than most, in fact. Yet she was joyful and a joy to be with. Her sister, who had more than most to be grateful for, was decidedly *not* grateful. Or joyful. Or fun to be with. Trust me. Not at all.

What made the difference? It was more than DNA. Perhaps some are naturally more sanguine than others about life and its vicissitudes, but that is an insufficient explanation. Myrtle was not born and destined to be a mean-spirited grouch. She gave in to it. She surrendered to self-pity so consistently for so long that it became the very nature of her life. She was not born to be miserable in her comfort. She was a self-made woman.

The fundamental difference between Ethel and Myrtle was gratitude, and the essential ingredient in the gratitude recipe is humility. Ethel was determined to play the hand she was dealt and to do it with joy. It never crossed her mind that she deserved better cards. Myrtle felt she deserved an infinitely better life than she got. Self-pity is the toxic stream that poisons the later years of so many seniors. As we age we can easily allow ourselves to compile a catalog of all the sacrifices we think we've made and the hardships we think we've endured.

Once we start down that dark staircase the next step is to calculate the material value of all that, and hey, we ought to have a return on all our years of investing. All the sweat and tears should mean something, something tangible at the end. Life owes us, and we want to see the check. When the check bounces, self-pitying, envious, angry senior citizens like Myrtle figure life turned out to be a rigged slot machine that just never paid off, all while ranting about entitled millennials who think they deserve the world.

Ethel's DNA probably contained some extra load of sweetness and light in there somewhere, but that cannot be the whole answer. Somewhere along the line Ethel made a decision. She was going to be joyful and grateful no matter her circumstance. She did not live in self-pity because her laboring-class husband died with no insurance. She did not inflict her grief and hurt and anger on everyone around her. She did not blame the world or her dead husband or God or whoever for her losses. Instead she counted her blessings and numbered among them other people's babies when she had none of her own and extra green beans when she could barely feed herself.

Gratitude is appealing at any age, but in our senior years it may be our last best hope of being attractive. But it takes humility. It's OK not to know everything. Seniors who let young people explain things to them are attractive. It's OK for us not to know who the hot bands are this hour. Let your grandchildren tell you how great they are as you nurse an inward, smug knowledge that whatever band they are talking about is nothing, worse than nothing, compared to Danny and the Juniors or The Crickets or Gladys Knight and the Pips, or, well, we could name them all night.

We know whichever band or solo artist they are talking about is not worthy to tie Elvis' shoes. Whichever talentless and plastic contemporary "country" singer, so called, that they gush about should not be mentioned in the same sentence with Bob Wills and the Texas Playboys. We know that.

Indeed, God knows that. But we need not point it out to them. We need to listen, pretend interest, and be grateful for the conversation.

When your son, not even out of his forties—and what could he possibly know about sports at that tender age anyway—wants to tell you all about how great this week's superstar is, try a little humility. Just listen while deep within you know, and the angels agree, that Larry Byrd, Willie Mays, Rocket Rod Laver, and Sugar Ray Robinson would defeat them, crush them actually, whoever they are. All that may be true, but you don't need to say it aloud. Let them talk about this week's heroes and villains. Humility listens. Humility is grateful they want to be with you and talk to you at all.

When you cannot make some piece of equipment work—some technological horror that you should not have to deal with and that promised to make your life easier and has not—humble yourself. Accept the help. Be grateful. Laugh at yourself. Then when you are all alone rant about stupid technology that has made our stupid world stupider and that should not have been foisted off on you in the first place because it is stupid, stupid, stupid. Go on and vent. Rant! You will feel better after the steam is released. Just remember to do it when you're alone. No one wants to hear it. Not even your spouse. Your spouse has asked God to let you know this, and I am His instrument.

When you eat Thanksgiving dinner at your daughter's house and she does not do it the way you always did it, which was, of course, the correct way, be grateful you are there at all. What? I can hear you object: She should be grateful for me. I raised her. Taught her to cook. I gave her life. She, not I, should be the grateful one, and this is not the dressing I taught her to make. She says it is not dressing at all. She has decided to make Kachchi Biryani instead of dressing. She got the recipe from a Bangladeshi cookbook a friend gave her. A friend? Not her mother? Not the recipe her mother gave her? Kachchi Biryani? It tastes like it. Do they celebrate Thanksgiving in Bangladesh? I don't *think* so.

Of course, you are right. On the other hand, would you rather be right or welcome at Thanksgiving? Praise the turkey. Compliment the cook. Eat the Biryani with as much gusto as possible. Be outspoken, even over-the-top, in your approbation. Then stop at Cracker Barrel on the way home. It will be filled with seniors avoiding each other's eyes. They will know. You will all know. Eat some dressing and giblet gravy and thank God you have money enough to pay for it and still buy an Anne Murray Christmas CD on the way out. When you get home have hot chocolate and enjoy Anne

Murray and be ever so happy you don't have to listen to Taylor Swift

This is not only about being with folks who do not remember and have no knowledge of who The Golden Bear was and who do not know Grace Kelly was the most beautiful actress/princess ever born. This is also about being with friends.

Do this the next time you go out with your posse for a wild night on the town, which would probably mean dinner at 4:30, followed by ice cream at Baskin Robbins, and home before dark.

Take a moment before you start all that late-night rockin' and rollin' and agree together not to talk about anything negative. Verbally, right out loud, make a covenant of fellowship for that night's festivities. Nobody gets to report on anything that hurts or no longer works as it once did. Any mention of surgery or medicine or doctors is right out. Grown children and their children who have become idiots cannot intrude on the evening. Don't ask. Don't tell. Make that the rule for that one night of crazy fun.

The only topics can be how wonderful it is to be alive and to be with each other and still recognize each other and know your own names most of the time. Share funny memories. Tell each other stories where you look dumb. Laugh lots. Laugh at yourselves. Laugh a bit too loudly and feel sorry for the young people around you who are embarrassed by "weird old people" acting like happy young people. Remember good fun stuff. Tell each other how great it is to be "among the very young at heart." Above all things remind each other that Frank Sinatra was right about one thing. You have a head start. When the waitress asks who Frank Sinatra was, tell her to google it and laugh some more because it is actually funny that you all know google is not a verb, but you say it anyway because you're so young and tech savvy.

The late evangelist Dr. Jack Gray, the founder of Bible Bowl, told me he wrote fifty thank-you notes every day.

"To whom?" I asked. "I cannot think of fifty people a day to thank."

"Then maybe you're not thankful enough," Jack said. "I just thank anybody that pops in my head. The more grateful you are, the easier it gets. The trash man, the mayor, the teller at the bank...whoever. Everybody loves getting a thank-you note. Not long. A few words like, 'Hey, I noticed what a great job you have been doing. Thank you.' Then sign your name. Just that. Maybe you're waiting to feel grateful before you act grateful. It works the other way. The more I thank people the more grateful I get."

I never reached Dr. Gray's fifty a day. In truth I never gave it a serious try, but his wisdom made me more intentional about thanking people. I started with family, then staff and employees. It gradually became easier and more natural. I have sent thousands of "thank you" and "good job" notes, texts, and emails over the years. Jack was right. It does get easier, and it makes you more grateful.

Some years ago Alison and I were running late to an event, and I was driving too fast in a pouring rain. I was concentrating on the rain and my destination instead of the speedometer. Of course I got stopped by a highway patrolman. When he told me how fast I was driving, I thanked him for stopping me.

I said, "Thank God you came along when you did. I could have had a terrible wreck."

"Are you being smart with me?" he asked.

"No," I said. "I am totally sincere. I wasn't paying attention. Thank you for stopping me. You may have saved our lives."

"I'm going to give you this ticket."

"I know. I'm not trying to argue my way out of it. I'm just grateful. I mean it. Thank you for doing your job."

"I am giving you this ticket," he insisted. "Do you understand me? You are getting a ticket. Here it is. I've written it. Take it."

I did take the ticket and thanked him one last time. He started away from the car and turned back. I lowered the window.

"I've been a Georgia highway patrolman for twelve years. I have never before, not one time, ever been thanked."

"Well," I said, "that's wrong. You should have been thanked. If no other speeder was or is grateful ever again, I am. Thank you."

"I'm not taking the ticket back."

"I understand."

"Just so you understand."

"I do, officer. I fully understand. Thank you again."

He went back to his car literally shaking his head. I like to think of him at a diner having coffee and a hamburger with some other cops and telling them that story. I see them shaking their heads just as he did. The fantasy makes me smile. Gratitude blesses people who need it, confuses the enemy of your soul, and touches the heart of God.

Gratitude comes naturally to few. The rest of us have to work at it. I have had to work at it, and I still do. Jack Gray was correct. Gratitude is not so much about feeling as it is about doing. Act grateful and eventually you will be more grateful. Along the way I've had others teach me gratitude, and I am still learning.

In 1982 Ghana was in a mess. The ruling junta was led by a ruthless and murderous Maoist dictator named J. J. Rawlings. Secret police who prowled the streets spied on everyone and even attacked some pastors in their pulpits. After curfew soldiers shot anyone on the streets, no questions asked. Petrol was outrageously expensive and rationed. The borders were closed so the shelves in the stores were empty. One could not buy bread or batteries. A paralyzed nation in the grip of hunger and under the boot of tyranny seemed an unlikely place to learn about gratitude.

Yet it was then and there where I saw the most authentic Christianity, the most genuine gratitude, and the most abandoned, unfettered praise in churches and families. Ghanaians in the early eighties were not the spoiled brats of today's Western church. They were not complaining about the music and the children's ministry or that the sermon went too long. They were filled with joy. They danced, literally danced, before the Lord and praised Him for small blessings. Their testimonies were not about winning the lottery "because God wants me rich." They were about how "the soldiers took my son two weeks ago, but he was released yesterday and is recovering very quickly." This would not be followed by fear and self-pity, but by applause and rejoicing and prayers for the soldiers to find the Lord.

One night I saw what humility and gratitude look like, what they really look like. I saw it up close and personal, and I will never forget it. I was staying in the home of a college president in Kumasi. In Ghana in 1982 that on-campus home was decidedly not the presidential mansion on an Ivy League campus. The whole college was hanging by a thread. The students worked in the college garden just so the little cafeteria would be able to feed them something. The electricity operated with all the dependability of a drunken Uber driver, and the faculty lived in small rundown cottages on the campus and worked for hardly more than room and board.

I found out that the oldest son's sixteenth birthday was to be celebrated one night; but, of course, I had no gift and no place to buy one. I did the only thing I could think of. I was at the end of my trip so I had one clean T-shirt left. I folded it neatly with a ten dollar bill (US) inside and put it in a plastic bag from a bookstore at Heathrow Airport. I was mortified that it was all I could do.

That night, after a supper of rice with scattered bits of chicken stirred in, the president's wife produced a small cake, hardly larger than a cinnamon bun, and we sang happy birthday to the young man. There were no presents, of course. There was a cake humiliated by its small size cut five ways, and everyone sang happy birthday. That was it. At that moment I presented my "gift," such as it was: a clean, used T-shirt and ten dollars in foreign currency.

His enthusiasm and gratitude were downright embarrassing. For their part, the president of that ragged little African college and his wife acted like the United States had sent them an ambassador with a congressional proclamation and a new car. They hugged me and thanked me extravagantly; then we all stood and sang a Ghanaian chorus about the unfailing goodness of God.

Gratitude in the face of adversity or need charms the heart of God. Self-pity is an accusation against God. If You were a better God, if You were better at the God-job, my life would be what I deserve. We can, of course, whine and moan about all we ought to have had. We can always do that. It comes naturally. We start life just like that. We can finish like that.

The most selfish, self-absorbed creature in the world is a baby. A baby cares nothing for his mother's fatigue or his father's sleep deprivation or for her parents' sex life. The baby cares only that it is wet and uncomfortable. Can't you sleep a little longer? the mother pleads. Nonsense! I'm hungry.

Up, I say, up and get that bottle going. You say you need sleep? I care naught about that. The bottle, slave. Get the bottle.

We begin life crying when things are not as we want them to be. That is not a good way to end life. Babies cry when they are wet or hungry or lonely and just want to be held. They cry a lot to express their unhappy condition. They sense intuitively that if they cry long enough, loudly enough, someone will come and fix it, whatever *it* is. They are so cute and cuddly, however, that no one holds it against them. Crying and wet and unhappy, a baby is still a cute little thing you just want to hold and hug and kiss on.

Old people? Not so much. We can die mean and angry and filled with self-pity; but if we die that way, we die old. Our best hope is to keep on giving and forgiving and being sweet and humble and grateful. Right to the end of this thing. We can keep on keeping on right up to the very moment when we die young...as old as possible.

EPILOGUE

THE MEMORIES OF my childhood, especially the better ones, are populated to a great extent by old people. My nomadic family, my parents and siblings and I, moved frequently because of my father's job changes. My father was never unemployed. He was a hard worker. He was just frequently employed. He would hear of a job in some far away exotic place such as California or Missouri or Florida, and off we would go.

All four of us children, remarkably, amidst all this coast-to-coast rambling, were born in the same small East Texas town of Commerce. I once joked with my mother that Texans must be like salmon; they come home to spawn. We never lived anywhere very long, and between stops we always came back to Texas and the old people. I remember, more than anything, the old people.

Both of my grandfathers were alcoholics. My father's father was a functioning alcoholic, a postmaster and small-time rancher. His drinking made him funny to us kids but not to his wife. My grandmother was sober, Church of Christ sober, and their marriage was a long chilly winter. They never divorced, but they were always miserable. This grandfather, whom we called Pop, had a fearsome bull named Domino and some white-faced Herefords and turkeys but no chickens.

Pop taught us to play poker, which outraged my grandmother. He also taught us naughty names for some of the cards. That made my mother angry. Pop made all the other adults angry, but he made us kids laugh. As a young child I was not exactly aware that Pop was an alcoholic. Not exactly, I guess. I certainly knew that the more beer and hard liquor he drank, the sillier and funnier he got.

My mother's father was not a functioning alcoholic. He was a drunk. He was extremely capable in many skills. He could build or fix or reupholster anything. He just could not stay sober. He was a binge drinker who spent much of his life in a deep and destructive addiction to alcohol. We kids called him PawPaw and his wife, my other grandmother, we called Granny. They separated because of his dreadful drinking, though they never divorced. I was not close to him.

We had distant aunts and uncles, such as Abe, who was a walker, something of a hobo who walked hundreds or thousands of miles every year. Wherever he stopped for a day or week or two he worked as a butcher. I was told by the other old people that behind a butcher counter Uncle Abe was an artist.

Uncle Abe would come walking in one day from no one knew where and then be gone like a puff of smoke.

My grandmother's brother, Uncle Lake, who sang bass, was a tiny man whose shiny cowboy boots were a boy's size. Lake's deep bass voice coming out of that diminutive body was remarkable.

Then there was my Uncle Chilton, who went up to Oklahoma one day and came home married to a quiet, full-blooded Cherokee woman. I do not remember ever hearing her speak. From my view as a small boy, Aunt Bea, as we knew her, seemed solemn and a bit forbidding. When the old people would gather to talk, Aunt Bea would sit outside the circle and take no part in the conversation.

I fondly remember an old man who was not in the family. His name was Mr. Salmon, and he lived just down the block from my grandmother in Commerce. He owned two huge wooden marionettes, Howdy Doody and Mr. Bluster. My junior brother and I were allowed to walk by ourselves from my Granny's house to Mr. Salmon's. He was very kind to us. He always had cookies on hand and was ever willing to take Howdy and Mr. Bluster down from their shelves and let us run our hands over their smooth wooden faces. Their lifelikeness stirred me somehow, and it seemed that Mr. Salmon understood my fascination. "Ain't they something special?" he would say, and I could only nod. The wooden puppets with mouths that moved up and down like nutcrackers were very nearly as mysterious as my Cherokee aunt.

Occasionally Uncle Wilfred would drive through Commerce or wherever we were at the time. He was our uncle only by marriage, and his wife had passed away. He was wealthy beyond anything I had ever seen in Commerce or Randolph. He drove a beautiful luxury car, perhaps a Cadillac, but I cannot remember for sure. By drove, I mean he drove all over the United States. In his eighties. All alone. He was always on his way to the Rose Bowl or to some PGA golf tournament or the Winter Olympics. Uncle Wilfred made a huge impression on me. He was sophisticated, well dressed, and successful. Whenever I questioned my mother about Uncle Wilfred, sometimes at great length, she would laugh about my interest in him. "You would like Wilfred," she would say, but I did not understand what she meant.

For one year my father lived and worked in Turkey. Dependents were not allowed to travel there at that time so my mother took us to live with my father's grandfather. Grandpa Rutland, as we called him, was a true, old-time Southern gentleman more like his birthplace of North Carolina than the Texas where he had lived most of his adult life. Even his house seemed as if it belonged in the Deep South. It had a huge front porch where Grandpa spent a great deal of his time. I have often thought how sweet and generous a person he must have been to let his grandson's wife and four rowdy kids move in for a whole year. On the other hand, his wife of whom I have no memory had died some years before, and I'm sure he must have been lonely.

It was at his house that we said grace at meals, not an everyday practice in our home. At the end of every table grace Grandpa Rutland always said, "Amen, brother Ben shot a goose and killed a hen." He was kind and quiet and very old. He adored my mother, and he wept when my father came home and we moved out.

My great grandmother on my mother's side was a tiny but volatile creature with an Irish temper that was never far beneath the surface. She could sing like a bird and play any stringed instrument ever invented. Her name was Lucy, but we called her Mammy. She was married to my great grandfather, whose real name was Tinsley Bledsoe, but to me he was Pappy. Of all the old people in my life, it was Pappy I adored. He had been a blacksmith in his youth then later the owner/operator of the country store in their tiny community of Randolph, Texas. He was loved and known by Randolph's citizenry as Mr. Tin. In my mind he was an old-time Texas hero like Sam Houston or Sul Ross.

I never heard Pappy say a negative word about anyone except one person, Liberace. When the old people would watch TV in the evenings, Pappy would watch too. *Gunsmoke. Ed Sullivan. The Hit Parade.* They were all fine, but when Liberace came on Pappy would snort, "Well, here comes old Lace on His Drawers," and he would shuffle out of the room. Pappy could not even stand to look at Liberace, and that his own womenfolk liked the famous pianist was a wonderment to him and a point of no small irritation.

They are all gone now. Not just the ones who were already old when I was a child. My own parents have passed away as well—my father at ninety-two and my mother a few months shy of ninety-nine. I am now in my seventies. How strange it is that I am now one of the old people. I am called Papa not Pappy, but it is a difference without a distinction. It seems I have become my own great grandfather.

Children without old people are impoverished. Children need to see what life near the finish line looks like. They need the unqualified love and the history and the stories and the silly addenda at the end of the table grace. Children without old people have an abbreviated life view.

Not too long ago, one of my grandsons texted me that his new favorite song was Riley Green's "I Wish Grandpas Never Died." It is a good song, but obviously that was not what he was communicating. He is a very young teenage boy facing up to the mortality of his beloved Papa. He thinks I am Sam Houston, and it is a small vanity which I allow. He wishes as we all do that people we love would never die. I wish I could talk to my old Pappy. I wish we could walk out to his shed in Randolph, Texas, and I could listen to him tell about his smithing tools. I wish I could hear him laugh and hear my Mammy play the guitar and sing "For the Love of Barbara Allen," or "Barbry Allen," as she sang it.

I wish Uncle Wilfred would drive into my driveway in his Caddy and tell me about attending the World Series. But he will not. He is gone. They all are. The old people of my childhood are no more. They all live in my memories and some of them in heaven.

When my Pappy died, I was about the age of my own grandson who texted me. I was a pallbearer at his funeral, and there yet again I was surrounded by old men. All the other bearers were quite elderly, and I remember being afraid they would drop Pappy's coffin.

It is strange to find oneself no longer the boy but the old man. It happened so quickly. It all fled by. One minute I was playing with a bow and arrow in a Chinaberry tree in my Pappy's front yard. The next moment my grandson is concerned about my death. With Riley Green he wishes I would not die. But I will. Death will come to me. Death comes to all of us. Death is as much a part of life as birth is. It has become something of a taboo subject in America. We do not talk about it. We hide it away from the kids and use euphemisms such as "passed on." We seem to be in a cultural covenant of denial. It is as if we have agreed that if we just do not talk about death, Riley Green's wish will come true and grandpas won't die.

We needn't be morbid about death, but we should be honest about it. We should prepare, write our wills, and provide for our families the best we can. We should be able to talk about it with our loved ones and assure them we are ready in every way, especially spiritually.

I said to my grandson, "I know what you're saying. You're saying you love me and you wish I would never die. I love you too, but you need to know this. Papa will die someday. Everybody dies. The thing is this: I'm not afraid. I am a Christian, and I will go heaven when I die."

All he said was, "I love you, Papa."

It was enough for that day.

I will never forget the first person I actually saw die. Carl was a fine Christian man, an old man, even older than I am now if that is to be imagined. At nearly ninety, Carl fell ill for what many said was the first time in his life. No one could even remember his ever having been ill. He worked in his own store carrying huge bags of seed and feed until three weeks before his death. After he had been in the hospital for some days, death seemed imminent, but his old body just could not seem to let go. I agreed to stay with him one night so his exhausted family could go home and get some sleep.

In the midnight quiet of the hospital, Carl lay breathing heavily almost in time to the rhythmic beeps of the machines to which he was attached. Suddenly he sat bolt upright in the bed, raised his arms, and looked at a blank hospital wall.

"Oh, beautiful!" he shouted and lay back down and died. I have never been afraid of death since that strange night. Carl must have gotten a peek through the door, and what he saw was beautiful.

Death is the doorway through which we must pass to move into the eternal. We live our earthly lives in the realm of time, and time races toward the finish line. As we age we think more about the end of life. At least we should. As seniors we know we are closer to the finish line than we are to the starting gun. Heaven is the realm of timelessness. The body we live in is the necessary and correct attire for the realm of time. It will not be suitable for timeless eternity. Death is the means by which we step into that realm and get dressed as we must be for that realm.

I can say to my grandson, "Someday I will have to leave this room. I will have to get out of this body and into the next one. This is natural. This is how it works. When that happens, go ahead and cry. It's OK to cry because you miss me. But it will be OK. It won't be nearly as long as you think, and I will see you again."

I have lived my life at full throttle. I have preached on every inhabited continent of the globe and in dozens of countries. It has been a great grand adventure so far, and it still is. I'm not through here. Not quite. I have loved a wonderful woman and love her yet. I was called, and I still am. He told me many years ago I was to be a preacher and a teacher and a writer, and I am still doing what He told me. Having said that, I do not dread the finish line.

As the old cowboy song says, "I'll eat when I'm hungry. I'll drink when I'm dry. If a tree don't fall on me, I'll live till I die."

When at last the tree in the yard comes crashing down, I will shout with Carl, "Oh, beautiful!" And I will not be afraid.

NOTES

Chapter 1

1. "Harvey 1950—10 Best Quotes," YouTube, accessed May 16, 2024, https://www.youtube.com/watch?v=E0WDCBOShRM.
2. "Young at Heart (Frank Sinatra Song)," Wikipedia, accessed May 11, 2024, https://en.wikipedia.org/wiki/Young_at_Heart_(Frank_Sinatra_song).

Chapter 2

1. William Shakespeare, *Macbeth*, Act 5, Scene 5, Folger Shakespeare Library, accessed April 11, 2024, https://shakespeare.mit.edu/macbeth/macbeth.5.5.html.

Chapter 9

1. Johnson Oatman Jr., "Count Your Blessings," Hymnary, accessed April 11, 2024, https://hymnary.org/text/when_upon_lifes_billows_you_are_tempest. Public domain.

Impacting lives through effective leadership, *New York Times* best-selling author Dr. Mark Rutland shares his decades of experience in leadership ranging from being a megachurch pastor to the president of two different universities. Gain practical, powerful, and inspirational knowledge through his perspective to navigate life as a twenty-first-century leader. As Dr. Rutland always says, "This podcast is about life, leadership, relationships, and faith."

DrMarkRutland.com

The Leader's Notebook **podcast is presented by**  globalservants

All revenue and royalties from Dr. Rutland's books
go directly to support the ministry of

© Austin Campbell

Global Servants is a nonprofit organization, founded by Dr. Mark and Alison Rutland, dedicated to empowering communities primarily in West Africa and Southeast Asia through girls' homes; education, clean water, and sanitation initiatives; and spreading the gospel of Jesus Christ. Global Servants operates House of Grace in Thailand and Ghana, providing safe homes, education, and a future for children at risk. Their mission is to spread love and hope and do all they can to improve the lives of people now and for generations to come across the globe.

globalservants.org

CONNECT WITH US!

@globalservants

Together, We Are Saving Little Girls For Big Destinies

BECOME A SPONSOR & CHANGE A LIFE!

To learn more about the work of House of Grace in Thailand and Ghana, and to explore the many ways you can get involved and make a meaningful difference in the lives of young girls, visit **globalservants.org** or scan the QR code below. Join us and become a cherished part of our global family.

All revenue and royalties from Dr. Rutland's books go directly to support the ministry of

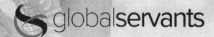

© Natthaya Rungsitdphiphat / Fay Inman